The Mother Tongue

A play

Alan Franks

Samuel French — London
New York - Toronto - Hollywood

Please see page iv for further copyright information

THE MOTHER TONGUE

First performed on 30 July, 1992, at Greenwich
Theatre, London, with the following cast:

Dorothy	Prunella Scales
Harriet	Gwen Taylor
Jeremy	Jamie Glover
Lettie	Bernice Stegers
Jo-Jo	Caroline Holdaway
Gerald	Robert McBain
Mr Bibby	James Bree

Directed by Richard Cottrell
Designed by Simon Higlett

The action takes place in the living-room of Harriet's
house in London

ACT I	Late afternoon in June
ACT II	Three weeks later

Time — the present

CHARACTERS

Dorothy The Mother of the title. Variously known as Nana to her grandson Jeremy, Mummy to her daughter Harriet, Dot to her suitor Gerald, and Mrs Cardale to the small public world beyond. She is in her early sixties but could pass for younger. She is smart and expensive and would expect to be nothing less, having spent the best part of thirty-five years as a company wife in the British community of Buenos Aires. Though widowed a year ago, she maintains standards (these include, above all, appearances), and is clearly having difficulty accommodating the liberal values of an England she no longer knows, and of a daughter whom perhaps she never did.

Harriet Fortyish, intelligent, beleaguered, underused, but bent on re-entry into working life. The trappings of conventional class (English boarding school) walked smack into the Sussex University of the 1960s, and the result remains a conflict. Her mother might call her sluttish if she used such words. Subjugation of her own career to that of her (frequently absent) husband Paul makes her wonder where she now stands.

Jeremy Often abbreviated — though never by his grandmother — to Jed. Eighteen. Probably bright enough for higher education, but the pursuit of his parents does not interest him. Getting by on charm and street wisdom, the product of a cultured home and the unculturing state school of the London borough where his parents chose to live. He might just give his mother cause to be perplexed by the results of *laissez-faire*. But he will soon be gone, and besides there is always his six-year-old brother Benji —"the boffin" — who is quietly about to atone for everything with a properly ambitious schooling made possible by his grandmother's money and desire.

Lettie A ball. American. Harriet's age. Wrestling with an eating problem and other areas of personal manageability. A force in the women's group which Harriet has recently joined. Up-front and glitter-hung, but definitely not a joke. Receiver and giver, with Harriet, of the warmth and support which show no signs of life between mother and daughter.

Jo-Jo Another member of the women's group, and effectively Lettie's apprentice. Madge Allsop to the American's Dame Edna. Working class. Northern. Struggling with everything — marriage, manners, language, self-help and Lettie.

Gerald A failure. Mid-fifties. Classless, but working on that one, even if he does come unstuck. A "career" too shady to be called chequered. Met Dot at the Kraelsheimers' art gallery in Fulham, cannot believe his luck, and who can blame him?

Mr Bibby An insurance man.

ACT I

Harriet's living-room. A late afternoon in June

The room is entered by a door UC, which leads in from the front hall. The room is fairly large, as the house must be, and is both hub and thorough-fare. Some knocking-through has taken place, for a kitchen and dining-room area form part of the general space. Everything that happens communally in this home happens here

We might be in Camden, or Wandsworth, but we are certainly not in Kensington, any more than we are in Sidcup. The pine may have been stripped, but there have since come the accretions of coffee mug rings and the general film of high usage. There are many books—used rather than decorative — and an air of productive disorder

As the CURTAIN *rises Harriet is on the phone, buoyant at first*

Harriet George, I know it's a lot of work, and that's exactly why I'm looking forward to it. So I'll expect the bike with the manuscript at about ten tomorrow. ... Yes, it was one of my specialisms. ... Benji has decided that my taking it on is a dereliction of maternal duty. ... No, not those exact words. ... I know he's only six. That's just it; if I don't get my brain working properly, he's going to overtake me. My mother, meanwhile, has slid back still further into girlhood, and this time she has really surpassed herself.

The doorbell rings

She must have heard us. ... In a taxi, I expect. She has yet to discover public transport. ... I don't know for how long. ... Yes, complete dread. ... It's a very long story ...

The doorbell rings again

And getting longer. ... Yes. Thanks. ... Bye. (*She hangs up*)

Harriet exits to the front door

(*Off*) Hallo, Mummy.
Dorothy (*off*) Darling, how lovely to see you.
Harriet (*off*) Leave the suitcases in the hall. Jeremy will take them up.
Dorothy (*off*) Lovely to have a resident porter.
Harriet (*off*) Come through.

Dorothy and Harriet enter with sundry bags

Despite being a new arrival, Dorothy makes herself instantly at home, more so than Harriet. Dorothy busies herself with small cleaning and tidying gestures that produce no visible results apart from the aggravation of her daughter

Dorothy Over an hour from the Kraelsheimers' to here. It is the limit.
Harriet Oh. Why?
Dorothy Because all the roads down here seem absolutely choked with buses. One hardly sees the need for quite so many.
Harriet Oh, I think they get used.
Dorothy If you say so, dear.
Harriet I must say, Mummy, you do seem to be taking this whole thing very calmly.
Dorothy What whole thing? Oh yes, well, you see in one way it could almost be said to be quite fortuitous.
Harriet I'm glad you can see it that way.
Dorothy Well, let's face it, dear, I think it would be pretty grim if we couldn't.
Harriet It's pretty grim as it is, if you ask me.
Dorothy I have always taken the view that when one door closes —
Harriet Except that it's not exactly a door, is it?
Dorothy What is not?
Harriet It's a house. A whole bloody house.
Dorothy I don't think language is a good idea, Harriet. Now then, I take it I am to have the nursery.
Harriet It's not the nursery; it's Benji's room. Benji is six, if you remember. Yes, you can have his room. He's in with Jed.
Dorothy Benji in with Jeremy? But that's new, isn't it?
Harriet Not particularly, no. We did it when Marie-France was here.

Dorothy Oh yes, the preggers one. Whatever became of her? Still preggers, I suppose.

Harriet No, actually.

Dorothy That at least was sensible.

Harriet She had the baby. Lives happily in, I think, Maida Vale.

Dorothy With the sound engineer, or whatever he was.

Harriet Yes. It was his baby too.

Dorothy One cannot help but feel sorry. They see the road ahead, and take a wrong turning, almost deliberately.

Harriet While Paul's away —

Dorothy Don't the boys scrap? Being in together?

Harriet Not more than usual.

Dorothy You and Veronica used to fight appallingly.

Harriet So did you and Daddy. But you still shared a room. Well, sort of.

Dorothy Now you're just being silly, I'm afraid.

Harriet While Paul's away, you can use our bathroom. We still haven't fixed the upstairs cistern.

Dorothy Still not fixed it?

Harriet No. No reason. Just not done it.

Dorothy Oh dear. Mrs Wiley will be dreadfully upset.

Harriet Who?

Dorothy You know, my "lady wot helps" at Kynance Terrace. The one we said looks so like Squirrel and the Zigger.

Harriet Did we?

Dorothy The nose especially, poor thing.

Harriet Why will she be dreadfully upset?

Dorothy She it was who when you were last round at the Estancia gave you the name of the little man who's apparently so cheap and comes from this sort of area.

Harriet I don't see how my cistern affects her.

Dorothy I suppose she likes to feel she's helping, that's all.

Harriet I thought she helped you every day.

Dorothy First thing tomorrow; top of the things-to-do slogger, I'm putting Mr Heaseman.

Harriet Who is Mr Heaseman?

Dorothy My plumber at Kynance. He won't mind coming across town.

Harriet Mummy ...

Dorothy I'll pay. Really awfully silly to have a loo that's *non operando*. I suppose you haven't ... erm .. in Benji's room.

Harriet No, it's still a tip.

Dorothy Never mind. The old girl's still a bit of a dab hand with the wallpaper. That goes on the list as well. Jolly good idea to have a list, is what I say.

Harriet That's very kind of you, Mummy.

Dorothy Still has her uses, what? Now then, tea.

Harriet Tea.

Dorothy Brought the maté. Nothing personal.

Harriet Course not.

Dorothy begins to make tea

So how long did you say it will be? I mean, roughly.

Dorothy I didn't say, darling. Did I?

Harriet Didn't you? Not that it matters.

Dorothy I don't think I would have said, if I don't know. Do you?

Harriet Do I what? Do I know?

Dorothy No. Do you think I would have said how long, if I don't know, is what I was saying. I think you'd be the first to agree that that has never been my style.

Harriet Right.

Dorothy So you see. Perfectly straightforward answer.

Harriet Which is ... ?

Dorothy I don't know.

Harriet That's fine. Fine.

Dorothy Is there something the matter, Harriet? You do seem most frightfully tense.

Harriet I'm fine.

Dorothy And how long did you say Paul is going to be away?

Harriet I didn't say.

Dorothy I know. That is why I was asking.

Harriet The answer is I don't know how long.

Dorothy Do you think that is wise?

Harriet I haven't actually thought about whether it's wise. I just don't know. And I don't know because he hasn't told me, and I expect he hasn't told me because he doesn't know because no-one's told him.

Dorothy Hardly satisfactory, one would have thought. I know things are very different now, but in my day, whenever Daddy was sent up country by the Frigorifico and I had to keep the home fires burning so to speak, they always had the decency to let me know how long he would be away.

Harriet Bully for you.

Dorothy If it's trust and good service you want — and by golly they got it from Daddy and me — you can't beat cards on the table.

Harriet ⎫ (*together*) Is what you say.
Dorothy ⎭

Dorothy And doesn't he ever ring? Daddy used to come on the wire all the time. Not for a chat but just to say, you know, A. Jones is OK, best wishes, A. Jones.

Harriet I don't thing the phones are very good in Bilwascarma.

Dorothy Well, I suppose you know best, dear.

Harriet I think it all depends on whether he's managed to get an interview with Violetta Chamorro and one of the d'Escoto brothers from the Ortega government.

Dorothy I say, you are well up, aren't you, Harriet.

Harriet Not desperately, no.

Dorothy All these names. Jolly impressive.

Harriet Then they plan to spend some time in Managua before going on to Washington.

Dorothy I must say; isn't it all rather sweet, when you think about it. Little Paulino.

Harriet In what way sweet?

Dorothy Well, I mean to say. All those fiendishly important things you see on the television. And there's little Paul in the middle of it. It seems so terribly ... well, grown up.

Harriet He is forty-three, Mummy.

Dorothy And when his name rolls up at the end. "Directed by —"

Harriet "Produced." It's producers who direct in current affairs.

Dorothy Well then they should jolly well say so. "By Paul Harrington."

Harriet Hartington. I'm Mrs Hartington, if you recall.

Dorothy You know what I mean.

Harriet It really is amazing how you keep getting his name wrong after all these years. It's almost as if his side of the family didn't exist.

Dorothy As though what?

Harriet Oh, nothing.

Dorothy Harriet, I do hope, most earnestly, that while we're ... that while I am here, you are not going to revert to that tiresome habit of starting to say something and then not finishing it, with no satisfactory explanation offered. I don't know where you picked it up from, but it really can vex one. Now then, a "cu'a".*

* NB "Cu'a" should be spoken as "cuppa" with the double "p" dropped out, in imitation of Mrs Wiley.

Harriet A what?

Dorothy "Cu'a". "Cu'a" char. Cuppa.

Harriet Oh. Thank you.

Dorothy That's Mrs Wiley. "Cu'a". Don't you remember, she kept saying it when you were last over at the Estancia, and you refused to catch my eye in case a fit of the giggles set in.

Harriet Oh yes.

Dorothy Mmmm. Delishwish. Still one of the old girl's fortes, wouldn't you say?

Harriet It's very nice, thank you.

Dorothy All I mean about Paul was how funny it sometimes is to think of that rather shy, fiendishly awkward boy you brought out with you to Buenos Aires in your last year at Sussex. And how he'd spent the entire flight mugging up on golf just so that he could talk to Daddy, and how Daddy had to lend him that baggy suit to go to the club.

Harriet And how Daddy came back so legless that he tried to flush his shirt down the loo.

Dorothy Oh, what nonsense.

Harriet Yes, he did. It wouldn't go down, so he started hitting it with the lavatory brush and shouting at it, and the maid thought he was being attacked by a burglar.

Dorothy If it amuses you dear.

Harriet It amused Paul, all right. Thought I'd dragged him eight thousand miles across the Atlantic to stay in a funny farm. You never remember those bits, do you?

Dorothy They were golden days, Harriet. Very special. The envy of everyone in the family. Biffo, Moisture, the Zigger, all the Squirrel cousins, they agreed that you and Veronica never knew how lucky you were.

Harriet How could we? We were locked away freezing in Suffolk most of the time being taught Latin by lesbians in gymslips.

Dorothy That is most ungrateful of you, Harriet.

Harriet To whom? You or them?

Dorothy The Latin stood you in very good stead for Spanish. Certainly well enough for you to flirt with, what was his name — the classically handsome one from Rosario whom we all agreed looked like Mario Lanza. You're not going red, are you, Harriet? Epiphanio, that was it. Epi. You know, I do believe you actually wrote to him in the lingo, didn't you?

Harriet You tell me. You never stopped snooping.

Dorothy Definitely gone red. Well, I never.

Harriet I have not gone red.

Dorothy If you say so, dear, but I'm not going to start rowing. You can educate the boys as you see fit, just as we did with you and Veronica. Grant you, it was jolly lucky we had the Frigger to foot the bill.

Harriet Actually, Mummy, do you know what that word really means?

Dorothy Of course.

Harriet Really means.

Dorothy Frigorifico.

Harriet Never mind.

Dorothy Doing it again, Harriet.

Harriet Doing what?

Dorothy Oh, nothing. Talking of the boys, where are they, in point of fact? It's pushing five.

Harriet Jed's gone to ... He's with friends. And Benji's at Gladstone's.

Dorothy Gladstone. Do I know him?

Harriet He knows you.

Dorothy Oh?

Harriet Yes. You ignored him solidly for two hours when you were last here.

Dorothy Hardly my style.

Harriet Anyway, that's where Benji is right now. Gladstone is one of his two little black friends, as the name might imply.

Dorothy Don't tell me the other one is called Disraeli or I shall hoot.

Harriet As a matter of fact it's Winston. Gladstone is in Benji's class.

Dorothy Goodness, I wonder how they can afford that. Cheap it is not.

Harriet The same way as I do.

Dorothy But —

Harriet Quite. Granny pays.

Dorothy As a matter of fact, Harriet, I'm awfully glad you brought that up. I'd been wanting to speak to you about it for some time.

Harriet You mean, you can't afford it anymore.

Dorothy Heavens, no. On the contrary. What with the house and everything. I think the old girl's finances are pretty healthy. You're happy with it, aren't you?

Harriet Well, yes.

Dorothy And Paul.

Harriet Yes.

Dorothy And I assume Benji is.

Harriet As far as I know.

Dorothy I mean to say, that Mr Simpson seems to do marvels. And Benji's voice hasn't well, hasn't ...

Harriet Gone?

Dorothy Like poor Jeremy's.

Harriet Mummy, what is it?

Dorothy It was Jeremy I was thinking of.

Harriet What about him?

Dorothy It does seem ever so slightly unfair — the boffin getting such a cracking good start. I mean, I'm sure you meant well when you, when you did it your way, with Jeremy. But is there nothing I can do to sort of help, or is it really too late? A crammer or something. There's meant to be a frightfully good one just round the corner from Kynance.

Harriet When I want to see good money spent on teaching Jed how to smoke dope in the lavatory with the sons of oil barons, I'll let you know.

Dorothy How very graceless, Harriet.

Harriet Jed's all right, Mummy. I keep telling you. He's perfectly happy. He doesn't want A levels.

Dorothy What does he want, then?

Harriet He wants money.

Dorothy laughs with an edge of derision

What's so amusing?

Dorothy Oh, forgive me. It's just so terribly, terribly funny.

Harriet How?

Dorothy Jeremy wanting to be rich.

Harriet Why is that funny?

Dorothy I was thinking of you, and Paul, and Sussex and everything. And Jeremy absolutely having to be taught Elsie Dee.

Harriet Who is Elsie Dee?

Dorothy You remember. It was Daddy's phrase. L.C.D. Lowest Common Denominator. And now all Jeremy wants is money.

Harriet I didn't say *all*. You're simply trying to mock.

Dorothy If you say so, dear.

Harriet Honestly, you've not been here half an hour and here we are arguing about schools again.

Dorothy I'm not aware of arguing at all. As a family we are extremely fortunate in not being given to rowing.

Harriet Oh yes. I almost forgot.

Dorothy I'm sorry I even mentioned the subject. I was only trying to help. I shall go and unpack.

Harriet I'm awfully sorry. I didn't mean to sound so ungrateful.

Dorothy The subject is closed. If I'm going to be a burden to you, I shall contact the Kraelsheimers at once and take them up on their offer.

Harriet The Kraelsheimers?

Dorothy Yes, the sweeties. They did say that if needs be they could alter the temporary arrangement into something less temporary.

Harriet But you can't possibly stay with the Kraelsheimers. You can't fart in their house without the burglar alarms going off. I bet they just wanted you as a free caretaker while they're off to Nassau or whatever it is.

Dorothy I suppose I have to confess if I am honest that the thought did cross my mind. I fear both you and I are the type who get too easily put upon. Besides which, I did think that an extra pair of hands might come in useful to you, what with all the au pairs having let you down so badly.

Harriet I'm managing.

Dorothy Of course the Kraelsheimers thought me a little foolhardy to come here.

Harriet Why is that?

Dorothy Well, you know. The shops and that sort of thing. The streets so crowded, and people one doesn't know.

Harriet Bit like Kensington.

Dorothy You know what I mean; I'm bound to say one still has very much the feeling of, how can I put it, camping. Have you and Paul never thought of moving?

Harriet We haven't discussed it.

Dorothy Daddy and I used to have regular pow-wows on the bricks and mortar front. Mind you, we were so lucky to have the Frigger behind us.

Harriet We're perfectly happy here.

Dorothy Are you?

Harriet For heaven's sake, yes.

Dorothy Happy. Are you and Paul happy, Harriet?

Harriet Yes.

Dorothy You know I've been worried.

Harriet I can't think why.

Dorothy When a woman starts working. It's often a sign.

Harriet A sign of what?

Dorothy It can be all sorts of things.

Harriet Well, it's not a sign of anything except that I wanted my professional life as well as ... as this one. And I'm *not* starting work, just taking it up again. Really, Mummy, I've told you all this.

Dorothy Do you mind Helen being so much younger than you are?

Harriet Helen?

Dorothy That is the name of the PA, or whatever it is they call them — the one who's gone overseas with Paul and his cameramen?

Harriet Yes. So what? What are you suggesting? I know her. She's been here to dinner. With her boyfriend.

Dorothy Oh. I'm sure she's most presentable.

Harriet And?

Dorothy Obviously she and Paul have to work closely; and they're in a strange country.

Harriet Yes?

Dorothy Well, he's human. Don't think the old girl hasn't knocked about a bit. You mustn't imagine that all men behave like Daddy.

Harriet Oh, I don't. I've seen some who manage to stop at just the half bottle of gin.

Dorothy That's unnecessary.

Harriet And so is all this. Honestly. Everything is perfectly all right.

Dorothy You know you can talk to me, Harriet. I think you'll agree it's always been cards on the table.

Harriet Jokers and all.

Dorothy I beg your pardon?

Harriet Oh, nothing.

Dorothy I think I'd better go and unpack. Then, if it's all right, I'll make a few phone calls. Moisture and the Squirrels. That sort of thing. Just to tell them A. Jones is OK.

Harriet What?

Dorothy Like we always do.

Harriet Yes, of course.

Dorothy And I'll do the meal tonight.

Harriet You don't have to bother.

Dorothy Then we must talk about money. You know what Mademoiselle Gourcuff used to tell me in Geneva: "*Des bons contes font des bons amis.*" Talking of which, don't let me forget to ring Mr Bibby tomorrow at Allied Provident. He's being an absolute treasure about getting the claim through quickly.

Harriet Oh, Mummy, honestly. What *were* you thinking of?

Dorothy A propos what?

Harriet The house, of course. Just think what you would have said if it had been me.

Dorothy I trust I should at least have been sympathetic.

Harriet Meaning that I'm not?

Dorothy Meaning that it goes to show what I have always maintained; one can never be too careful.

Harriet But it's an absolute disaster.

Dorothy Only if you let it be. I repeat, when one door closes —

Jeremy enters

Jeremy (*speaking as he enters*) Another one opens and in comes Jed to see his old Nana.

Dorothy Jeremy, *querido amorsino*.

They kiss

And how is Grandma's favourite little man?

Jeremy He is well pissed.

Harriet Jed, for Heaven's sake.

Jeremy You did ask. He is slaughtered, gutted, arseholed. Like Gramps.

Dorothy Is this necessary?

Jeremy No, just fun.

Dorothy I see.

Jeremy Relax, Nana. Make yourself at home.

Dorothy I think that's a lovely welcome.

Jeremy What I find is, there's very few people left in this world who — how shall I put it — actually make the lavatory smell better after they've used it than it did before. Know what I'm driving at?

Dorothy Well, I think so, dear. One is trying.

Jeremy This *is* Nan's home now, innit?

Harriet It would appear so.

Dorothy Well, just for the briefest of whiles.

Jeremy Oh, not *too* brief, I hope.

Harriet Who can say?

Jeremy How brief then?

Harriet This has yet to be established.

Dorothy I beg your pardon, dear?

Harriet Oh, nothing.

Dorothy Jeremy, does Harriet make a habit of saying, "Oh, nothing" to you all the time?

Jeremy Not that I've noticed, Nana. Why?

Dorothy I just wondered.

Harriet If you would rather I made myself scarce while I am under discussion, I can easily arrange it.

Jeremy No, Mum. Hang around.

Harriet It's almost time I picked Benji up from Gladstone's.

Dorothy (*to Jeremy*) The little black one.

Jeremy Oh, *as* the ace of spades.

Harriet Jeremy, please.

Jeremy But it's ever so hard to be a proper snob without a nice dollop of racism.

Harriet (*genuinely amused, to the puzzlement of Dorothy*) This is true.

Jeremy I was just about to ask Nana to what we owe the pleasure.

Dorothy Of?

Jeremy Of having you here.

Harriet Her house ——

Jeremy Yeah, I know all about that. I mean how come not over with ——

Harriet Veronica.

Jeremy Yeah, with Auntie V.

Dorothy You sound disappointed.

Jeremy In what?

Dorothy Well, in Veronica, I suppose.

Jeremy No, don't get me wrong. I'm well glad you're here.

Dorothy But.

Jeremy Well, I mean Auntie V. and that dirty great big place of theirs on Richmond Hill.

Harriet More up Mummy's street, you mean.

Jeremy I'm not having a go, Mum, honest.

Harriet I know, darling.

Jeremy Just that ... well. You know.

Dorothy Oh, I expect that Veronica has her reasons.

Harriet And Frank.

Dorothy Mmmm?

Harriet Frank. Your son-in-law.

Dorothy Yes. You know, it's never a good idea to presume on your children.

Jeremy Look, all I meant was why Auntie V. wasn't sort of ——

Dorothy Rallying round?

Jeremy If you like.

Dorothy Oh, I expect she and Frank are up to their ears in entertaining.

Harriet Actually, there is a reason.

Dorothy Very possibly, dear. But if it entails you speaking disparagingly about another member of the family — and I include Frank ——

Harriet He doesn't.

Dorothy Then that's his misfortune. As I say, if there are going to be words about another member of the family, then thank you but not in my earshot.

Jeremy Chill out, girls.

Harriet As I say, there is an explanation.

Dorothy Now I'm afraid you're repeating yourself, Harriet. I repeat ——

Harriet Although it may not appeal to you very much.

Dorothy In that case, it is just as well that the subject is closed.

Harriet Rather like the door.

Jeremy What is this door?

Dorothy Harriet was speaking metaphysically.

Harriet Phorically.

Dorothy I'm sorry?

Harriet I think you meant metaphorically, even though I was meaning physically.

Dorothy If you say so, dear.

Jeremy Still don't get it.

Dorothy Unfortunately, Jeremy, neither you nor your grandmother have been blessed with Harriet's education.

Harriet Please don't start that again, Mummy.

Dorothy I am not aware of starting anything, dear.

Jeremy You two on about schools, again?

Harriet I'm afraid so.

Dorothy Why afraid?

Jeremy Probably been discussing jobs and all.

Harriet That too.

Jeremy Oh dear.

Harriet No, not yours, Jeremy.

Jeremy Oh?

Harriet Mine.

Jeremy Right. My turn next, I expect, then.

Harriet Mummy seems to have got it into her head that I am somehow starting out in professional life for the first time.

Jeremy Must be getting you mixed up with me.

Harriet I have tried to point out to her that there is nothing new about me editing for Hardings, and that I did it for years before Benji was born.

Jeremy I was wild in them days.

Harriet You know, actually going into offices, seeing authors, having budget meetings, that sort of thing. She, on the other hand, seems to deny the existence of such years.

Dorothy You do slightly make it all sound as though you were trying to play at being a man.

Harriet Oh, for Christ's sake.

Dorothy Harriet, *pas devant.*

Jeremy French I do have, Nana.

Dorothy I grant you I was overseas at the time.

Jeremy You was overseas and Gramps was seas over.

Dorothy Not funny or clever, Jeremy.

Harriet More sad, I would say.

Dorothy I also have to concede that there have been, well, changes.

Jeremy How d'you mean?

Dorothy In the way of what goes. Standards.

Jeremy Oh yeah, we've been an outrageous little country while you've been gone.

Dorothy And what is it like to have what I believe is called a working mother? As if motherhood were not a full-time profession in its own right.

Jeremy Eh? Well, it's ... I mean, I got a brilliant Mum, that's all. I'm well proud of her. Yeah, great.

Dorothy Not after something, is he, Harriet?

Jeremy Just telling the truth.

Dorothy And do you never, how can I say, aspire to something of that sort yourself?

Jeremy Ah, so it *is* one of those, is it?

Dorothy One of what, dear?

Jeremy You know; my turn next. What do we do about Jeremy, like.

Dorothy Your mother and I were merely ——

Harriet No, not your mother. Your grandmother.
Jeremy Look, if you want to discuss me, I can make myself scarce and all.
Harriet No need, Jeremy. I must get a move on. Mummy, I'm taking your suitcases up.
Dorothy Not necessary, dear.
Jeremy I'll do that, Mum.
Dorothy It is a man's job, Harriet.
Harriet Just the thing for me in that case.
Jeremy Please, Mum.
Harriet No, you sit and talk to Mummy.
Jeremy Go on.
Dorothy Harriet.
Harriet (*as she goes*) No, please don't begrudge me the right to feel useful.

Harriet exits

Dorothy Ah well, *chacun à son modus vivendi*, I suppose.
Jeremy This is it.

With Harriet absent, Dorothy and Jeremy fall, as if by established habit, into the ritual exchanges of grandmother/grandson

Dorothy Now then, let's have a proper look at you. Have we grown?
Jeremy Give us a break, Nana.
Dorothy I do believe we have. Breaking a few hearts already I shouldn't wonder.
Jeremy No, legs, mostly.
Dorothy Oh dear.
Jeremy Yeah, well they ask for it.
Dorothy Not getting into fights again, are we?
Jeremy Only when the need arises. You know how it is.
Dorothy Is this wise, Jeremy?
Jeremy Case of having to.
Dorothy You seem to have a nasty cut on the left of your face. Not shaving, is it?
Jeremy No, Stanley knife.
Dorothy Oh.

Jeremy Sideboards done it. A bloke called Sideboards.
Dorothy And who, if one may ask, is Sideboards?
Jeremy Merchant banker.
Dorothy Isn't that rather out of character?
Jeremy No, merchant banker. Wanker.
Dorothy I'm afraid you sometimes rather lose me, dear.
Jeremy Pratt, jerk, berk.
Dorothy A-ha.
Jeremy We was down the club.
Dorothy A club indeed. We have gone up in the world.
Jeremy It's an armpit. Don't half get some slags down there.
Dorothy It sounds most frightfully demi-monde, Jeremy. Precisely what manner of club might this be?
Jeremy D.S.S.
Dorothy Is that a sort of community centre?
Jeremy Divorced, separated and singles.
Dorothy I see.
Jeremy Well, I'm single ain't I?
Dorothy Unless you've been keeping some colossal secret from me, yes.
Jeremy Sideboards isn't, you see. Married, but flung out, so whenever I'm round, it shows him up as soiled goods.
Dorothy And presumably being considerably your senior.
Jeremy There's that too. He's well past the sell-by date. Plus he hasn't got the patter. It's all stuff about cars he's done up and how he's on the brink of a major break business-wise. In a word, Nana, he lacks class.
Dorothy And you don't.
Jeremy How could I, with you having bombarded my genetic make-up with all those toff chromosomes?
Dorothy Is that what I did?
Jeremy I'm grossed out on class, and there's no way it's not going to show. Same with the boffin.
Dorothy So Benji is classy too, is he?
Jeremy Benji is not just classy. Benji is positively expensive.
Dorothy I see. And that's one up on classy, is it?
Jeremy No, it just means he costs a lot.
Dorothy There I am bound to agree.
Jeremy I know what you sometimes think. The voice and that. But I got it sussed and I can alternate at will between modes, thus: May I press you to a *petit four*, Camilla?

Dorothy Very passable, dear. And what does Camilla say at this point?
Jeremy Naff off, usually.
Dorothy A-ha.
Jeremy Which I am more than glad to do, her being a total bicycle off of
whose saddle a man could easily find himself infected.
Dorothy How simply ghastly. I don't believe a single word you say.
Jeremy Like that, is it?

Harriet enters

Dorothy Do you, Harriet?
Harriet Do I what?
Dorothy Believe what Jeremy says.
Harriet What does he say?
Dorothy Oh, all sorts of things.
Harriet Why shouldn't I?
Dorothy Such antics.
Harriet Go on.
Dorothy I don't think you'd believe me, dear.
Harriet Believe you, or believe him?
Dorothy I would have thought that was obvious, dear.
Harriet Right.
Dorothy Now then, Jeremy, wash those grubby little paws and then you
may have one of your grandma's special scones.
Jeremy What, the big Kensington numbers with the flash jam? Yeah, ta.
Dorothy And I think there's still a "cu'a" in the pot.
Jeremy You taking the mick, Nana?
Dorothy Oh that. Just one of the old girl's silly jokes. My daily help at
Kynance. Harriet is *au fait*, aren't you, dear?
Harriet Apparently.
Dorothy You're joining us, yes?
Harriet I really should fetch Benji.
Dorothy Just a quickie. I think you'll agree it's rather scrummy.
Harriet Oh all right. Thank you.
Dorothy Well then. *Saldades.*
Harriet *Glasnost.*

Silence

So here we are then.

Dorothy Here we are. Mmmm. Maté tea, proper scones — and secs.
Jeremy And what, Nana?
Dorothy Secs, silly boy; short for second helpings. That one goes way
back to St Hilly's.
Jeremy Oh, right.
Dorothy You two, honestly.

Silence

Jeremy So. Good here, innit?
Dorothy I was saying to Moisture only the other day that I can think of
no more heartening sight than that of a family pulling together.
Jeremy Which one is Moisture, Nana? I get confused.
Harriet Moisture is the strategic postal orders one.
Jeremy What?
Harriet A sudden windfall for you and Benji just before she happens to
need a bed in London.
Dorothy Oh, surely not, dear.
Jeremy Aren't they, you know, rallying round, the Squirrels?
Dorothy Oh certainly, Jeremy. Except that with the best will in the world,
Shropshire is, well, so frightfully not near anywhere.
Harriet Quite handy for Cheshire, I'm told.
Dorothy Now that, Harriet, was a Jeremy sort of line.
Jeremy What I say, Nana, is shame about the house, eh?
Dorothy What house is that, dear?
Jeremy How many you got?
Dorothy Slightly silly question.
Jeremy I mean, the Estancia.
Dorothy Oh. My news. Yes. I thought for a moment you meant this one.
Harriet Why this one?
Dorothy Surely that does not require an explanation.
Harriet Isn't it good enough for you?
Dorothy It's not me I was thinking of, dear.
Harriet Well, there's a thing.
Dorothy I though that perhaps you and Paul might have, well, outgrown
it.
Harriet It's perfectly big enough. Most of the time.
Dorothy I suppose it's more the area.
Harriet Then why not say so?

Dorothy Well, they are so, so ... sort of ... joined together, aren't they.

Harriet If this is another attempt to have us move, Mummy, thanks but no.

Dorothy I was only thinking that now that you and Paul have, as it were, made your point ——

Harriet What point?

Dorothy I think you know what I mean, dear.

Harriet It's not a point. It's a home. My home, I think. And if you don't like it, then you can try Veronica's.

Dorothy What an extraordinary outburst, Harriet.

Harriet It's such control.

Dorothy I beg your pardon.

Harriet Oh, you wouldn't understand.

Dorothy A little *self*-control wouldn't come amiss.

Harriet You haven't got a clue, have you?

Dorothy Perhaps the matter is best considered closed.

Harriet Yes, just seal it up.

Dorothy A case of least said soonest mended, I think.

Harriet How I hate that stupid saying.

Dorothy It's always stood me in perfectly good stead.

Harriet It legitimates secrecy and deviousness.

Dorothy In that case, rather like "Oh, nothing." Except perhaps a little more forthright.

Harriet I'm going to fetch Benji.

Dorothy Very well, dear.

Harriet Look, I'm ... I'm sorry, all right?

Dorothy Perfectly.

Jeremy Why don't the two of you just give each other a hug or something?

Dorothy I am perfectly game.

Jeremy You know, just a sort of no-hard-feelings hug.

Harriet I'm sorry, but I really am in a rush now. (*She moves towards the door*)

Jeremy In that case ... (*He walks over to Harriet and places an emphatic kiss on her cheek*)

Harriet What was that for, Jeremy?

Jeremy It's a kiss, that's what for.

Harriet But I'll only be a few minutes.

Jeremy It's 'cos you're a brilliant mum, all right?

Harriet Well, thank you, darling. I don't know what to say.

Jeremy Don't say nothing. It was a wotsit, a non-conditional one.
Dorothy You mean there are other sorts?
Harriet You are a lovely boy.

Jeremy extends his jaw and closes his eyes, hoping for a reciprocal kiss. Harriet kisses him a little stiffly, like someone whose favoured means of communication is not physical

Harriet exits

Dorothy Perhaps she is not used to being the recipient of a kiss at present.
Jeremy You what?
Dorothy Oh, nothing.
Jeremy Cheer up, Nana.
Dorothy What's the matter?
Jeremy With me, nothing. It's you.
Dorothy But I'm fine, Jeremy. Absolutely fine.
Jeremy You can't be fine.
Dorothy But I tell you that, in spite of everything, I am fine.
Jeremy Not allowed here.
Dorothy What is not allowed?
Jeremy Being fine. You have to be more specific.
Dorothy But why?
Jeremy 'Cos otherwise it shows you're not in touch with your thoughts and feelings.
Dorothy My thoughts and feelings. But I am perfectly in touch with them, and I can assure you that they are fine, too.
Jeremy You see, what fine really stands for is fucked up, insecure, neurotic and egocentric.
Dorothy I really must ask you not to use language. I can only think you do it to wilfully offend. Where *does* it come from?
Jeremy Mum, mostly.
Dorothy Oh, honestly.
Jeremy Well, from the group.
Dorothy What group?
Jeremy Women's group. If you say you're fine, they're on to you like a pack of jaguars.
Dorothy And who are these women?
Jeremy Friends of Mum's.

Dorothy What sort of friends?

Jeremy I dunno. I don't get involved. I believe in letting her have her space.

Dorothy And yet you plainly have the rough drift of it.

Jeremy Well, obviously one has to take a certain basic interest in what's going on in the household.

Dorothy And are they new friends?

Jeremy Oh, yeah. All pretty recent.

Dorothy I rather thought that might be the case.

Jeremy Mind, I say friends, but if you ask me, I reckon they all give each other a pretty hard time. I mean, I come in from a gig the other night, and there was what you could call an atmosphere. Half of them was in tears with their heads in their hands and the ones that weren't in tears were pointing their fingers at the ones who were, like they wanted to make it worse. And then they all start rounding on each other and telling them they're being judgemental.

Dorothy Judgemental.

Jeremy Yeah, that's another thing you're not allowed to be.

Dorothy I see ...

Jeremy But then there's a little one crying behind her hair who suddenly roars back into the frame and says they're all guilty of displacement.

Dorothy Displacement.

Jeremy Now there's language for you, Nana.

Dorothy But what does it mean?

Jeremy It means you know you're a bollocks, and that the others know you know you're a bollocks, but you're not having it, so you make out it's one of the others who's a bollocks instead.

Dorothy Please, Jeremy.

Jeremy But this little one, she's out of order 'cos she's gone judgemental on the rest, and gets accused of dumping.

Dorothy Dumping.

Jeremy Same as displacement, only less subtle. She also picks up a few penalty points for losing her temper. But she's a clever one and she's got the jargon sussed, and so she comes back at them with "It's not temper, it's justifiable anger," which makes it OK.

Dorothy And Harriet is in the middle of all this?

Jeremy Oh, Mum's in there batting, as far as I can tell.

Dorothy And all this happens here in the house?

Jeremy Lately, yes.

Dorothy But why here?

Jeremy 'Cos Mum's got the biggest gaff, I suppose. Plus, there's no bloke about.

Dorothy What about you?

Jeremy As I say, I just came in at the tail end.

Dorothy So what do you do?

Jeremy I do what any normal geezer would do. I nick the scotch and go upstairs to watch the golf. I don't enjoy seeing people suffer. I do what Gramps would have done.

Dorothy I think that little joke has had more than a fair innings. And are they, so to speak, married, these women?

Jeremy Search me, but I know what you're getting to.

Dorothy Do you?

Jeremy Yeah. You mean, are they dykes?

Dorothy Jeremy.

Jeremy I would have to pass on that one. There's quite a lot of touching; you know, long touching when the hand stays on the shoulder and slides off like it didn't really want to go. But then I do that myself. What I'd say, Nana, is that there's maybe just one pair of Osh Kosh dungarees too many for a normal bloke to feel entirely at his ease. But that's as far as I'd go on that one.

Dorothy And does Harriet seem to be happy with all these friends?

Jeremy Well, she's on the phone to them a lot. And she's reading their sort of books. There you are ... (*He passes her two books from the sideboard*)

Dorothy glances at the books without dignifying them through too close a contact, and puts them down beside her

Dorothy *Women Who Love Too Much* ... *My Mother Myself*. What engaging titles.

Jeremy I think Mum's changed

Dorothy How changed?

Jeremy Well, this talk for a start. She does it with me and all.

Dorothy Really?

Jeremy Little things. Little phrases.

Dorothy What, you mean she calls you, whatever it was, judgemental?

Jeremy No, not that, 'cos I tend to keep my opinions to myself. Other things like, "It's your choice". Whenever I complain about anything, it's always, "It's your choice". I call it stripped pine jargon for tough titties. She hates that.

Dorothy Now tell me, Jeremy, do you wilfully rile her? What I believe you would call wind her up?

Jeremy No more than you do, Nana.

Dorothy And what is that supposed to mean?

Jeremy Just that.

Dorothy But as a family ——

Jeremy As a family, we're lumbered with each other and we take it from there.

Dorothy I'm disappointed in you.

Jeremy No, you're not. You're disappointed in Mum.

Dorothy I am not. I have given her every opportunity.

Jeremy It's Mum that's disappointed in me, just as I'm disappointed in her and she's disappointed in you.

Dorothy *Meo pobre filinho*. What fiendish bilge you do sometimes talk.

Jeremy Not bilge. We're all disappointed 'cos there's not the right amount of us in the other one. Too much, maybe, or too little, but not the right amount. So what do we do? We run and hide in the things we say.

Dorothy We do what?

Jeremy You just done it.

Dorothy I have?

Jeremy The Spanish and that. We go where we feel comfortable. Mum's into judgemental, I'm into whatever it is I'm into, and you're into the Frigger and all that.

Dorothy The Frigger. What about the Frigger? It's simply the word we all used. All Gramp's colleagues.

Jeremy Exactly.

Dorothy Do you actually know what the word means?

Jeremy Me? Yeah, I know what Frigger means. It's short for Frigorifico.

Dorothy Thank you. I do rather worry about her.

Jeremy That's your job. 'Specially since Gramps dropped off the hooks, I mean, passed on.

Dorothy Aren't you worried about her?

Jeremy Tell the truth, I've decided the time has come to let her make her own mistakes. Course, I've tried to guide them both when they needed me, but you can't lead their lives for them, can you?

Dorothy But seriously.

Jeremy Seriously. For all I know, she's having a nervous breakdown.

Dorothy She seems so preoccupied all the time, as if there's something going on — something away from where she really is.

Jeremy But you could say that about a lot of people.

Dorothy About Paul, for example.

Jeremy Oh no, not Dad. He's right into his thing.

Dorothy Yes, but that thing is not here, is it?

Jeremy Not a lot, I suppose, no.

Dorothy Which might explain something about why Harriet is the way she is.

Jeremy Ah, it's always been like that. We're one of those families in which Mum takes all the little decisions, like how to get Benji's hearing fixed, and Dad handles the big ones, like what's to do about the Labour Party.

Dorothy Not exactly one for letting charity begin at home, is he?

Jeremy Come to the point, Nana; are you suggesting that Dad's putting it about?

Dorothy That he is putting what about?

Jeremy That he's knocking that Helen woman off? Now are you?

Dorothy I wouldn't have put it quite like that.

Jeremy Course you wouldn't. But I'll tell you this. Dad is not a cruel man. If he was slipping Helen one, he'd be the last person in world to hurt Mum by letting her know.

Dorothy Oh, Jeremy, a woman has her ways of knowing these things.

Jeremy What, you mean underpants and that?

Dorothy Please.

Jeremy I know what Dad gets up to and what he doesn't get up to.

Dorothy In that case you succeed where Harriet and I have signally failed.

Jeremy It's easy.

Dorothy You mean he tells you?

Jeremy No, I open his mail.

Dorothy Don't be ridiculous.

Jeremy Well, not exactly open it.

Dorothy What then?

Jeremy I let the steam do the work.

Dorothy The steam!

Jeremy I must say, it's been a lot easier since Mum got that new plastic kettle.

Dorothy You mean, you snoop?

Jeremy Not if it's a boring old begging letter from his school; but even some of the phone bills can be a rattling good read. It's all a matter of how you approach it.

Dorothy I can only say it's jolly fortunate I don't believe a word you say.

Jeremy Fortunate for you, maybe, but not for Dad.

Dorothy Really, Jeremy.

Jeremy Some of the new gum's a bit of a bastard, but mostly it's a piece of cake.

Dorothy I suppose you picked it up from that school.

Jeremy No, from Mum.

Dorothy From Harriet?

Jeremy I saw her one night through the kitchen door, years ago.

Dorothy If I thought that was true, I think I should have to speak to her about it.

Jeremy I already have.

Dorothy And what did she say?

Jeremy To wait until the gum was really moist.

Dorothy I don't believe it.

Jeremy She's really nifty.

Dorothy And I suppose *she* acquired the habit at those frightful digs in Brighton.

Jeremy No. She said she picked it up from you in B.A.

Dorothy Not true, not true.

Jeremy She said you did it on Gramps' mail.

Dorothy This does not even bear discussion.

Jeremy As a family, Nana, we do tend to steam each other's letters open.

Dorothy I suddenly begin to fear for my privacy in this household.

Jeremy Yeah. Me, too.

Lettie and Jo-Jo, carrying plasic grocery bags, enter on a wind of their own. This blows them past Jeremy and Dorothy and straight into the cul-de-sac of the kitchen. This is not a matter of prerogative, or ousting, since they are too preoccupied for anything quite so confrontational, but rather of routine. Physically at least, the domestic initiative has suddenly passed to the younger players. Their activity is not yet feverish. They have simply put down a marker, in the form of their plastic food bags, to which they will return in due course

Lettie So don't take your shit away with you. Leave it here, OK?

Jo-Jo OK.

Lettie You say OK, honey, but will you do it?
Jo-Jo Yes. I've said yes.
Lettie You gotta get real.
Dorothy Good-afternoon.
Jeremy Hallo.
Lettie No Hat?
Dorothy Oh. Should one?
Lettie Not back yet, huh?
Jo-Jo She never stops, does she?
Dorothy As a family ——
Lettie Forget family.
Dorothy Ah.
Lettie I always say forget family. Right, Jo-Jo?
Jo-Jo Right, Lettie.
Dorothy Jeremy ...
Jeremy Yeah?
Dorothy I don't think we've been introduced.
Jeremy Me neither.
Dorothy I am ——
Jeremy This is Nana.
Jo-Jo Hallo, Nana.
Lettie We love you, Nana.
Dorothy I see.
Lettie Tough love's what you get.
Dorothy I don't know what to say.
Jeremy And that's Lettie, and that's Jo-Jo.
Lettie You're in the right place.
Dorothy That is most reassuring. Thank you.
Jo-Jo Are you from here?
Dorothy Do you mean from here, here?
Jo-Jo Yes.
Dorothy Well, in a manner of speaking.
Jo-Jo Been here long?
Dorothy Yes and no, really.
Lettie We're on dependency tonight.
Dorothy That sounds most diverting.
Jeremy Oh Jesus.
Lettie Did you bring the dependency tapes?
Jo-Jo Got them here.

Jeremy Roll over, Beethoven.
Jo-Jo So what's with you?
Jeremy I'm fine.
Dorothy Not allowed, surely.
Lettie Well, that's right. Stands for ——
Dorothy And you? How about you?
Lettie Me?
Dorothy Have you been here long?
Lettie We just arrived. So where's Hat?
Dorothy I'm not sure that we have anyone here of that name. Although I can check. Jeremy?
Jeremy They mean Mum, Nana.
Dorothy Silly me. And you are, again?
Jo-Jo Jo-Jo.
Dorothy One would be tempted to say how singular. Except that, it's ... it's not, is it? A-ha-ha-ha.
Lettie Jo-Jo's in therapy.
Dorothy How frightfully clever of you. I gather that sort of thing takes years of training.
Lettie No. *In* it.
Dorothy What, you mean, now?
Jo-Jo Oh come on, Lettie.
Lettie What have I told you? You're as sick as your secrets.
Jo-Jo I'm in therapy.
Dorothy Well, since cards are on the table, I'm in antiques. At least, one dabbles. You know how it is.
Jo-Jo No, as a matter of fact, I don't know.
Dorothy Ah.
Lettie I didn't say be rude to the lady, Jo-Jo.
Jo-Jo I'm not being rude. I just said, no, I don't know how it is. You say to get honest and I'm saying I don't know what an antique looks like, OK?
Dorothy Over the years it has been my observation, *vis-à-vis* therapy, that once it has all, so to speak, come out, it can be so very difficult to, well, put it back in again.
Lettie Are you group?
Dorothy Oh, I think we all are to some extent, don't you?
Lettie Who did you say you are?
Dorothy I don't think I did.

Jeremy She's Nana.
Lettie OK.
Dorothy Well, Nana as in ... Jeremy.
Lettie Uh-huh.
Jeremy She's Mum's mum. She's my gran.
Jo-Jo So, *not* group.
Lettie Holy shit.
Dorothy I take it you are friends of my daughter's and that she is expecting you.
Lettie Well, I'd say more we're expecting her.
Dorothy In that case, snap.
Lettie You what?
Dorothy Snap.
Lettie I don't get it.
Dorothy It's a little word we say when, for example, we find that we share one another's experiences.
Lettie OK.
Dorothy In point of fact, it's a card game.
Lettie A card game. OK.
Dorothy Now then, would anyone care for a ——
Jeremy Cup of tea.
Lettie Thanks, but I don't drink.
Dorothy Erm. Josephine?
Jo-Jo Er ...
Lettie Just get it out, Jo-Jo.
Jo-Jo Right. No. Thank you. I mean, later.
Dorothy What about some scones? My grandson is rather partial, but I dare say ——
Jeremy And then we can all have secs.
Lettie We can what?
Jeremy That one goes way back to St Hilly's.
Lettie Thanks, but I'll take a rain check. I'm in O.A.
Dorothy O ... A?
Lettie Overeaters. Anonymous.
Dorothy Quite.
Lettie You seem puzzled.
Dorothy No, no. It was merely the anonymity which caught me somewhat unawares.
Jo-Jo Hadn't we better get on, Lettie?

Lettie Sure.

Dorothy So soon? Well then, it's been a great pleasure to have made your acquaintance.

Jo-Jo Are you going?

Dorothy Why, not as far as I know. That is, not imminently.

Lettie We gotta get set up for group.

Dorothy I understand.

Jo-Jo Do you?

Dorothy I've heard so much about you from other members of my family.

Lettie Oh.

Dorothy Yes.

Lettie In that case, snap.

Lettie and Jo-Jo confirm their temporary ascendancy by moving into the kitchen area and unloading the food which they have brought. Dorothy, as if above such territorial ambition, retreats to the opposite side of the living room. Jeremy follows, and they sit

The following sequences between Lettie and Jo-Jo on the one hand, and Dorothy and Jeremy on the other, are enacted quite independently of one another

Dorothy Now then, Jeremy, where were we?

Jeremy I think I was about ... there, and you were slightly to the right and moving towards the kitchen area.

Dorothy I am bound to say, they do rather act as if they owned the place. I shall have to have a word with Harriet.

Jeremy I think they already have.

Lettie So how are you feeling?

Jo-Jo Like I wish that woman wasn't here.

Lettie That's not a feeling. Anyway, I'm handling her.

Dorothy I think I saw the Americana off rather effectively, don't you, dear?

Jeremy Eh? Oh, yeah. Yeah.

Jo-Jo Weird.

Lettie You're feeling weird?

Jo-Jo No. *She's* weird.

Dorothy Particularly over the rather ticklish question of her eating. Far, far too young for a figure like that. One almost feels sorry.

Jeremy But not quite.

Jo-Jo Do you suppose she's stopping?

Lettie Don't project.

Jo-Jo I was only asking.

Lettie This evening is another day.

Dorothy You know, our very dear Dr Juarez used to have a rather imaginative treatment for that sort of thing.

Jeremy What was that then?

Dorothy Not in polite company, I fear.

Jeremy Oh, shagging.

Dorothy Fortunately I didn't hear that. Let us just say that some have rather more difficulty than others in obtaining the treatment.

Lettie You still feared up about letting go?

Jo-Jo Letting go?

Lettie Of Bruce.

Jo-Jo Brian.

Lettie Brian, then.

Dorothy I'm sure you get my drift.

Lettie You gotta put him down.

Jo-Jo You make him sound like a dog.

Lettie So do you, honey. So do you.

Jo-Jo I thought it was no put-downs.

Lettie Detach with love. You gotta let go. Look at me.

Jo-Jo I am.

Dorothy Nature can be cruelly uneven in her favours.

Lettie I gotta detach from cookies. Sure it's hard I ain't binged for three months. Yeah, I go looney tunes, but I'm clean.

Jo-Jo Now you're making him sound like a biscuit.

Dorothy If we could just retrieve a few of my goodies from our friends.

Jeremy I don't think they're into nicking stuff.

Dorothy I wasn't implying. (*She girds herself for a foray*)

Lettie There's no growth without pain. Take Hairnet Monica.

Jo-Jo Monica from the estate?

Lettie Right.

Jo-Jo But she doesn't wear a hairnet.

Lettie Not now, she doesn't. She's grown.

Dorothy (*to Lettie and Jo-Jo*) Excuse me. I say. Yoo-hoo.

Lettie (*to Dorothy*) You rang?

Dorothy I wondered if you could see your way to giving the Chocolate Olivers a fair wind.

Lettie Can I help?
Dorothy The ones from Horrids. In ... in my pile.
Jo-Jo I think she means can you sling over the green bag.
Lettie Sure.
Dorothy Thank you so much.
Lettie No problem.
Dorothy I'm indebted. (*She returns to Jeremy*)
Jo-Jo She's a monster is that one.
Lettie You're libelling monsters, honey.
Jo-Jo Harriet deserves better.
Lettie Never mind. It's all meant.
Jo-Jo But why?
Lettie Because Hat needs to do some work in that area.
Jo-Jo Poor love.
Lettie Remember, Jo-Jo. The child is mother to the woman. Can't you I.D. with that?
Jo-Jo No.
Lettie OK. Keep it simple. It means Hat's at risk.
Dorothy They really do appear to have just taken over the place.
Jeremy I wouldn't let it get to you, Nana.
Dorothy I was thinking of Harriet.
Jeremy Course you were.
Dorothy I suppose it would make them happy if we simply went and squatted in the nursery with a Thermos flask.
Jeremy Yeah, probably.
Dorothy I'm bound to say, you do seem remarkably unconcerned.
Jeremy Not my business, is it?
Dorothy Isn't it?
Jeremy I let go, don't I?
Dorothy You let go.
Jeremy Yeah.
Lettie Hey, we got a commitment.
Jo-Jo What's that?
Lettie The dependency tapes.
Jo-Jo I said, we've got them.
Lettie What about the copies?
Jo-Jo Oh, God.
Lettie Remember? Hairnet Monica said she'd do the literature and we said we'd copy the tapes.

Jo-Jo But what's the time?
Lettie Time we did it. We promised.
Jo-Jo But where?
Lettie Hat said to do it upstairs on Paul's dubbing deck.
Jo-Jo But what about the food?
Lettie Food's almost done.
Jo-Jo What about *her*?
Lettie What are you feared up for?
Jo-Jo Don't you think I should watch it?
Lettie No you don't. You and me gotta talk. C'mon.

Lettie and Jo-Jo move from the kitchen area into the neutral buffer zone of floor. Dorothy's radar registers a move of significance

Dorothy Ah.
Lettie We're just going upstairs.
Jeremy It's your choice.
Dorothy You'll find it's just up the stairs.
Lettie Oh, if someone comes in ...
Dorothy It could well be my daughter.
Lettie It might be Hairnet Monica. She does the literature.
Dorothy Another fearfully bright one. Any messages?
Lettie Just hi, we're upstairs.
Dorothy I think we can manage that, Jeremy.
Jeremy No sweat.
Lettie I don't want for her to be sitting around on her fanny.
Dorothy Never a good idea. Hairnet Monica. So, no huge problems of
  identity there.
Lettie Hang loose.
Dorothy We shall try.

Lettie and Jo-Jo exit

Dorothy Jeremy.
Jeremy Nana.
Dorothy Now then, where had we got to before our little foreign
  invasion?
Jeremy Jo-Jo's not foreign, Nana.
Dorothy Perhaps not technically. I think you were just telling me about
  work.

Jeremy I don't think I was.
Dorothy In that case you were just about to.
Jeremy Was I?
Dorothy Definitely. What actually is work these days, if one dare ask?

Dorothy now settles into the natural rhythms of food preparation. Her rights of occupation are clearly beyond question. Moreover, Jeremy's cautions are eclipsed by a theme dear to himself: namely, himself. Which was the whole idea

Jeremy Little bit of this, little bit of that.
Dorothy Jeremy, what *are* you going to do?
Jeremy You mean be? What I'm actually going to be?
Dorothy Yes.
Jeremy Cult figure.
Dorothy Just like that?
Jeremy No, no, there's a lot of work in it.
Dorothy What sort of cult figure?
Jeremy I am at present firing on a number of fronts, Nana.
Dorothy Is the group still going?
Jeremy Band.
Dorothy Oh dear. By whom?
Jeremy No, it's a band. Post-modernist. Group means Mum. Band means me.
Dorothy Are you doing well?
Jeremy Breaking even. There have been a number of personnel changes owing to unforeseen clashes of temperament.
Dorothy That seems a shame. And how many of you were there?
Jeremy Six.
Dorothy And after the re-shuffle?
Jeremy One. In fact, Nana, I think I could be said to have gone solo.
Dorothy So, failing the cult figure ambition, anything else in mind?
Jeremy Estate agent.
Dorothy Goodness, that's rather a leap, isn't it?
Jeremy No. Same thing. You just stand there peddling shit and getting seriously wealthy. Even these days.
Dorothy I say, you simply must meet my friend Gerald. He'll be terribly tickled to hear you say that.
Jeremy Who's Gerald?

Dorothy Just a friend.

Jeremy Nana, you've not gone red, have you?

Dorothy No. Why?

Jeremy My eyes are reporting to me in fairly emphatic terms a progressive pinkening of the boat race.

Dorothy Now you're just being silly, I'm afraid.

Jeremy In fact, I do believe we might be in a fancy man situation here.

Dorothy What a terrible expression.

Jeremy Now then, where's this Gerald live?

Dorothy To tell you the truth, I'm not entirely certain.

Jeremy So where d'you meet him?

Dorothy At the Kraelsheimers' new gallery in Fulham.

Jeremy So quite swank then.

Dorothy *Fino*, definitely.

Jeremy He's what?

Dorothy What we used to call *fino*. It means simply, well, you know, like fine, except ...

Jeremy Classy.

Dorothy That will do.

Jeremy Like you.

Dorothy No, I would be *fin*a. Feminine ending, Jeremy, if you had any Latin.

Jeremy If you're going to have a fella, he's got to be a good one. I mean that.

Dorothy I know you do, and bless you for it. As a matter of fact, I know it sounds odd, but he reminds me ever so slightly of Gramps.

Jeremy Not d.t.'s is it?

Dorothy I didn't hear that.

Jeremy Work, does he?

Dorothy Oh, almost certainly.

Jeremy What's his line then?

Dorothy His what, dear?

Jeremy His business. You know, job.

Dorothy Oh, one doesn't actually ask that sort of thing.

Jeremy But you just asked me.

Dorothy Slightly different.

Jeremy Oh, right.

Dorothy There are clients. He has clients.

Jeremy And when is it you've asked him to come?

Dorothy Oh soon.
Jeremy When, soon?
Dorothy Well, now really.
Jeremy Now.
Dorothy Nowish.
Jeremy You mean today?
Dorothy Yes. I think it was today.
Jeremy Sounds very casual.
Dorothy Oh no. More informal, I would say.
Jeremy He coming for dinner?
Dorothy Not as such.
Jeremy He's not shacking up, is he?
Dorothy Oh dear, no.
Jeremy I find it so hard to tell what goes these days. So you are actually expecting him nowish.
Dorothy Ishish. Like me, he was brought up with the good manners to know that if someone says six o'clock, they really mean six-thirty. I know that might sound quaint to some.
Jeremy Yeah. Today it's called being late. And did you say six?

Lettie and Jo-Jo enter. Seeing Dorothy in command of strategic heights, they have no choice but to loiter, albeit purposefully, at the mouth of the kitchen area

Lettie That's the beauty of it; you really can leave your shit here.
Jo-Jo Right.
Lettie You don't have to cart the stuff around with you anymore. You're freed from all that. Can you imagine what that means; how that feels?
Dorothy That's twice they've come in, and twice they've been discussing the same thing. I know the cistern is out of commission, but one does start to wonder.
Jo-Jo No Hairnet Monica?
Dorothy Not that we've noticed.
Jo-Jo She did say six.
Jeremy Perhaps she means six-thirty.
Lettie Hat's back.
Dorothy So the milliner has delivered at long last.
Lettie Eh?
Dorothy Oh, nothing.

Lettie She's upstairs.

Dorothy I'd sort of got there by process of elimination.

Lettie Benji's not well.

Dorothy That comes as no surprise.

Lettie She might be able to use a hand.

Dorothy Thank you for letting me know.

Lettie (*attempting a fresh push into the war zone, and outnumbering Dorothy by two to one*) Do you think we could just —

Dorothy (*standing her ground*) I'm ever so tied up with my paupiettes de veau.

Lettie Lady, we had the food to finish.

Jeremy I'll go up.

Dorothy No, Jeremy. You were being such a help with the paupiettes.

Jeremy Was I?

Dorothy And I'll need you for my Charlotte Russe.

Lettie We did have the food to finish.

Dorothy My grandson and I have been admiring your novel approach to the quiche.

Jo-Jo Flan.

Dorothy I haven't made a quiche for donkey's years.

Jo-Jo Flan.

Dorothy Quiche, I think you'll find.

Jo-Jo It's a flan.

During the following the dispute moves up a gear, into what could easily pass for a jostle

  Also during the following Harriet enters, more than usually stressed, and glimpses the end of the dispute

Dorothy If I could perhaps have the merest hint of elbow room.

Jo-Jo She has *so* much work to do.

Dorothy There I am bound to agree.

Lettie You are *not* a polite person.

Jeremy Girls, please?

Harriet What on earth is going on?

Jo-Jo Your mother ...

Lettie No, Jo-Jo.

Dorothy These people ...

Jeremy No, Nana.
Harriet Jeremy.
Jeremy Yeah?
Harriet What have you been doing?
Jeremy Is that a you-plural question, Mum?
Harriet Please don't be insolent.
Jeremy Not being.
Dorothy There was a tiny disagreement over the question of a quiche.
Jo-Jo Flan.
Dorothy I would hate you to get the idea that it was anything other than thoroughly civil.
Harriet Lettie, Jo-Jo, I'm so sorry if I was a little short with you upstairs.
Jo-Jo That's all right, love.
Lettie We love you, Hat.
Dorothy She seems to have found the right one at last.
Harriet (*with real warmth*) It's really lovely to see you both.

Harriet hugs Lettie and Jo-Jo

And I'm sorry about all this.
Lettie But it's not your fault. Don't pick up the blame.
Dorothy I too would like to apologize.
Jeremy Good God.
Harriet What for, Mummy?
Dorothy For having insisted on accuracy.
Harriet Well, there we are then. Everyone is sorry. Isn't that marvellous. If Jeremy could find something to be sorry for, we would sort of have a full house. Jeremy?
Jeremy Oh, I expect something will turn up soon.
Dorothy He has been a credit to us, Harriet. Where is Benji?
Harriet I've put him to bed. He's not feeling at all well.
Dorothy Oh, the poor boffin. And I did so want to say hallo. Shall I just nip up?
Harriet No. Thank you. You'll only over-excite him. I mean, he throws up at the slightest thing.
Dorothy Probably something they gave him at Gladstone's.
Harriet Haven't you unpacked yet?
Dorothy You do seem most frightfully brusque, dear. Is everything all right?

Harriet Well, I have a sickening child and a pile of manuscripts the height of Big Ben.

Dorothy But not too busy to entertain.

Harriet That's my business. Lettie, Jo-Jo, I feel I should offer you an explanation.

Dorothy If there's any left over when you've finished, dear, I wouldn't say no.

Harriet I shall come to you presently.

Lettie You're doing great, honey.

Harriet Mummy — that is, my mother — is here for an indefinite period while her own accommodation is sorted out. She was forced to move when ——

Dorothy Harriet.

Harriet — when her house in Kensington was destroyed by fire.

Dorothy I don't think they want to get bogged down in details, dear.

Harriet I have told her she may of course have the run of this house for the time she is here. That is my decision. (*To Dorothy*) Mummy, these are two very dear friends of mine. They are frequently here at my invitation. This evening we will be joined by other friends. Is all this clear?

Dorothy I believe Hairnet Monica is due.

Harriet Mummy, don't do it.

Dorothy Do what, dear?

Harriet What you are doing.

Lettie Good, Hat.

Harriet I do not want to behave in this way.

Dorothy It's your choice.

Harriet I think we will have to talk.

Dorothy And what, pray, is this?

Harriet It's games.

Lettie Hang in there.

Harriet Sick games.

Dorothy I have told you that if I am in any way an encumbrance, you are at perfect liberty ——

Harriet What liberty?

Dorothy What do you mean, "What liberty"?

Harriet Oh, nothing.

Dorothy Please not "Oh, nothing".

Harriet I'm so sorry, Lettie.

Lettie Don't pick up the guilt, honey.

Dorothy It's all right, Harriet. I am not angry.

Lettie No, she's handed it over.

Dorothy It's just that, earlier, we seemed to agree that I would be doing the meal tonight.

Harriet Did we?

Dorothy That was certainly my understanding.

Harriet I'm sorry.

Dorothy And I said that precisely because it seemed to me unreasonable to expect you to cater for someone you had never met.

Jeremy So he *is* coming to dinner.

Dorothy I told you, Jeremy. Not as such.

Jeremy Don't get it.

Harriet Is who coming?

Jeremy It's a bloke.

Dorothy Jeremy.

Jeremy But he is a bloke. In the sense that he's a fella. True.

Dorothy Oh, but these words.

Jeremy Companion.

Dorothy Er ...

Jeremy Escort?

Dorothy Hardly.

Jeremy Gentleman caller.

Dorothy No.

Jeremy Toy boy.

Harriet Quiet, Jeremy.

Dorothy He has been an invaluable help, and I thought that a good moment to show the flag would be when I was, as it were, holding the fort.

Harriet Have you any plans this evening, Jeremy, which you feel we ought to know about?

Jeremy Not as such.

Harriet That's something.

Jeremy In point of fact, I think the action's here, Mum.

Harriet No friends you'd care to wheel in on the off-chance?

Jeremy It's all right, I'll share Gerald.

Harriet I see. Gerald. And who, precisely, if one might ask, is Gerald?

Dorothy Goodness, dear, you are sounding exactly like my mother.

Lettie Sher-yit.

Dorothy Whenever she said who, what she really meant was what.

Jeremy He's quite swank and he's got clients but not d.t.'s and ——

Doorbell

—— and he's here.
Dorothy Ah.
Jeremy Nana, old son, I think we just ran out of ishes.

For the briefest of instants any one of the five might be a candidate for the answering job

Dorothy I'll go.
Harriet It might just be for me. You never know.
Jeremy Sounds like a Gerald ring to me.

Dorothy is first from the traps, and goes from the room towards the front door, patting her already perfectly presentable coiffure as if to check for blemishes

The others settle for inertia. Harriet looks at Jeremy in an information-seeking way, but Jeremy has eyes only for his feet. Guilt seems to have flowed his way as well

Jo-Jo It could be Monica.
Harriet She's got a key.
Lettie OK.
Harriet I'm so sorry, Lettie.
Lettie Stop that.

Dorothy returns in full sail with Gerald in tow

There are various brands of soundless wincing from the onlookers. He is laden with chocolates and champagne and has worked on his entrance, which aims at the grandiose mode. Dorothy is preening in sympathy. Pride and apprehension are locked in battle for the control of her features

Jeremy No hairnet.
Dorothy Harriet, this is Gerald. Gerald, my daughter Harriet. My grandson Jeremy. Jeremy, Gerald.

Jeremy Glad to meet you, Gerald.

Gerald Gerry, please. Lovely. Lovely. Lovely place. Oh yes. Oh yes. Tricky to find, mind. Got one of those cabbies who did his knowlege in the jungle. Ha-ha-ha. (*To Harriet*) Heard so much about you from Dot. (*To Dorothy*) Isn't that right, poppet? Well, here we are then. A pair of the old Plonco del Fizzeroonie to kick us off, ay what? And a small offering from the delectable fayre of Monsieur Suchard. It may be Swiss, but by golly, it's sweet, what. A ha-ha-ha! And finally, for the lady of the house ...

Dorothy thinks this is her, but it turns out to be Harriet. Gerald whips a bunch of collapsible flowers from his sleeve. Harriet has no choice but to receive it. Gerald's laughter, which is standard accompaniment for all his own gags, spreads to Jeremy, who finds it all genuinely funny; then to Dorothy, whose amusement starts polite and unsure, but becomes enthusiastic. Little here for Lettie except bemusement, while Jo-Jo, who is not beyond contagion, is simultaneously laughing at and laughing with Gerald. As all four fall into their respective responses, Harriet's wince matures to a shudder. She removes herself as far as space permits

Lettie Sher-yit.

Gerald's flowers discover an extra skill —flashing

Harriet (*to no-one and everyone*) Oh, dear God!

Black-out after the first few flashes. The flashing continues, even more conspicuous in the darkness

CURTAIN

ACT II

Three weeks later

As the CURTAIN *rises Harriet, confronted by a mountain of work, is at the table. Lettie and Jo-Jo are about to leave*

Lettie So we'll let you get on, honey.

Harriet It was lovely of you both to drop by.

Lettie That's some pile of literature you got there.

Harriet It is rather, isn't it.

Lettie And then we'll be round to pick you up for the meeting, for half six. You got your mother to baby-sit Benji, right?

Harriet And Jeremy. And ... that man.

Jo-Jo You'd have thought they were old enough to look after themselves of an evening.

Harriet No, I mean they're staying in with her.

Jo-Jo I know, pet.

Lettie Act adult, Jo-Jo.

Jo-Jo I was only trying to enliven. You said I was to graft some animation on to my declared self.

Harriet He seems to be round here almost as often as he's not.

Lettie D'you suppose he's a gold-digger?

Harriet The man couldn't lift a shovel. God, he's useless.

Lettie What do they do?

Harriet I don't know. I think she's teaching him Spanish, and telling him about antiques. And they seem to talk about property prices. But they stop whenever I come in. Even Jeremy's gone shifty. I don't know.

Lettie And how is it making you feel?

Harriet Feel? It makes me feel paralyzed. It makes me feel I could ask my voice to talk, or my body to move, and neither of them would obey.

Jo-Jo I've been there. I've got that T-shirt.

Lettie That's a passé phrase, Jo-Jo.

Harriet Somehow I just don't seem to be able to get down to my own work. I get myself mentally prepared, I stare at it for hours, I start, and then the concentration just packs up and disappears. Do you know what I mean?

Jo-Jo I've walked that corridor and all.

Harriet I can't hold on to the sentences. I have them, and then they slip away like a bar of soap. Tell me, Lettie, do you suppose I might be suffering from re-entry trauma?

Lettie If you mean do you get traumatized whenever your mother re-enters the room, then I would say you're a victim of the syndrome, yeah.

Harriet She makes me feel as if I'm doing something I shouldn't the whole time. Or else not doing something I should. And I start to act guilty, even think guilty, although I know I'm not. Sometimes, when I'm sitting here — I know this sounds absurd — I feel as if she's inside me, kicking and growing, and controlling me from within. And she gets so huge and strong that she has to come out, or else something terrible will happen. But then I can't do it. And the kicking and growing goes on, until she spreads up and down the whole length of me. Do you understand?

Jo-Jo It's actually quite a common occurrence in Bingley.

Lettie Jo-Jo.

Jo-Jo I'm serious, love. I'm saying I understand. I really do. Don't you?

Lettie Of course I do.

Harriet And that man. She's besotted. The first one to show an interest since she's been alone and she turns him into a demi-god. It's obscene.

Jo-Jo D'you suppose they're bonking?

Harriet What, in this house? Oh, please.

Jo-Jo It has to be a possibility.

Lettie It's not our business, Jo-Jo. Is there any movement in the home front, Hat? I mean her home.

Harriet I don't know. Whenever I raise the subject, she takes it as a personal attack and plays the martyr.

Lettie That figures.

Harriet In what way?

Lettie Tell her, Jo-Jo.

Jo-Jo It's a device for transferring the sense of guilt from her to you. For making *you* feel bad about *her* not having a place.

Lettie Well, that's right.

Harriet How d'you know?

Lettie It's common. Our Dorothy is not as unique as she would have you believe.

Harriet I think it's that awful, I don't know what it is, bogus stoicism I suppose, that most makes me want to scream. All the stuff about how when one door closes ——

Gerald and Jeremy enter

Gerald Another one opens and in come the boys.

Harriet Hallo.

Gerald Afternoon, girlies. So it's off on the tear tonight, is it?

Jo-Jo I beg your pardon?

Gerald You know, slipping the leash, making whoopee while your menfolk play Cinders.

Jeremy I don't think they're all married, Gez.

Gerald Oh. Right you are. Well, you know what I mean. Erm, no sign of Dot?

Harriet Mummy is taking Benji to Gladstone's. We are expecting her back at any moment.

Gerald I say, poppet, what a Mum you've got, eh? All that fetching and minding and not so much as a whimper. I expect you sometimes wonder how you'd manage without her. Wouldn't you say, girls? And you know what? I've got bags of identification with you regarding that one. In point of fact, I have I D by the jolly old wagonload. Know why? I'll tell you. Because I sometimes wonder how I'd manage myself. I'd wager most young mums would give their eye teeth for a gran like that. And I'll tell you for why. See, what we have here is a lady — and I am using the term advisedly, mind — who is not only very much at home when at home, if you get my drift, but also an enhancement to all concerned when, so to speak, on the town. So, I think we all do rather well, really. No, Jeremy?

Jeremy Didn't mean to disturb you, Mum. We're just off down the club. We'll be back to Benji-sit. What's the matter? Something not good enough? You can say. Sorry, girls.

Dorothy enters

Dorothy I say, what a crowd.

Gerald Dot, *amorado*.

Jeremy Feminine ending, Gez.

Dorothy I do hope I'm not disturbing anything.

Jeremy No, we're just on our way out from under Mum's feet.
Dorothy That's very considerate of you, dear. Nice to find some sensitivity about.
Lettie We were going too, weren't we, Jo-Jo.
Jo-Jo Yes.
Dorothy Oh please, not on my account.
Lettie On our own actually; and Hat's. Come on, Jo-Jo.
Harriet I'll be ready about half-past six.
Lettie See you later, Hat.
Harriet And thanks so much for ... for this afternoon.
Jo-Jo No problem. Ta-ra, love.
Dorothy And do come again when we're all a little less frantic.
Lettie Oh, we will.

Lettie and Jo-Jo exit

Gerald Your ears must have been burning, Dot.
Dorothy Not that I noticed, Gerald. Should they have been?
Gerald Ooo, the compliments that were flying in here.
Dorothy Compliments?
Harriet From him.
Dorothy You know, Gerald, you really are far more generous than I deserve. Isn't that so, Jeremy?
Jeremy No.
Dorothy *Que chico simpático!*
Jeremy Me and Gerald's just off down the club, Nana.
Dorothy I think you mean Gerald and I are just off down the club, don't you?
Jeremy Yeah, that too.
Dorothy Well, try not to be too bad an influence on him, if that's at all possible.
Gerald You'll be all right here, Dot?
Dorothy Fortunately we are perfectly at ease with our own company.
Harriet Oh, how true.
Jeremy You fit, Gez?
Gerald Butcher's dog, dear boy, butcher's dog.
Jeremy We are going to have to do something about your language. (*To Harriet and Dorothy*) See you later.
Gerald *Buenos noches*, all.

Dorothy *Días.*
Gerald Quite so.

Jeremy and Gerald exit

Dorothy Well then.
Harriet Well then.
Dorothy Busy?
Harriet Not really. Only five hundred and seventy-three pages of manuscript to edit by tomorrow morning.
Dorothy That does sound an awful lot.
Harriet It is.
Dorothy And jolly closely typed.
Harriet Isn't it.
Dorothy You would have thought ...
Harriet No, Mummy.
Dorothy Anything interesting?
Harriet Christ and Marx in the evolution of liberation theology in Latin America.
Dorothy Ah yes.
Harriet The bike's coming at ten-thirty in the morning.
Dorothy So I'll do the Benji run, shall I?
Harriet Hmmmm?
Dorothy Take Benji to school.
Harriet Yes.
Dorothy As per usual for the last three weeks.
Harriet Thank you.
Dorothy You don't mind me asking, do you?
Harriet Asking what?
Dorothy If it's all right to take the boffin to school?
Harriet Of course I don't mind you asking.
Dorothy You are his mother.
Harriet So what?
Dorothy Some mothers quite like to know what their children are up to.
Harriet Some never stop.
Dorothy Meaning?
Harriet Oh, nothing.

Silence

Dorothy He's at Gladstone's at the moment.

Harriet Yes.

Dorothy I just thought I'd keep you in the picture.

Harriet Thank you.

Dorothy Gladstone's father was there.

Harriet Good Lord.

Dorothy He's really rather nice.

Harriet Amazing, isn't it.

Dorothy One of those very black negroes which you do get. But I would say definitely *fino*. If one weren't looking at him, one could well assume that he were otherwise than he is.

Harriet Yes, he went to Rugby.

Dorothy For the merest moment I suspected that there might have been a hint of oop north.

Harriet Oh.

Dorothy And then I thought, no, to be black and northern would have been too much of a trial for anyone. We had quite a chat.

Harriet Good.

Dorothy Fearfully well informed.

Harriet Isn't he.

Dorothy Rather a cut above *la mujer*, one suspects.

Harriet Yes, love's funny like that.

Dorothy There I agree. One does see what on the surface appear to be the most grizzly mismatches.

Harriet Doesn't one just.

Dorothy But if they're happy.

Harriet Quite.

Dorothy In his case I would have thought there must be at least a degree of social embarrassment. Still, it's not for us to say, is it?

Harriet No.

Dorothy I shall be picking Benji up in exactly one hour.

Harriet Fine.

Dorothy After Mr Bibby's been.

Harriet Who?

Dorothy Mr Bibby. From Allied Provident.

Harriet Oh, yes.

Dorothy After that I have a hairdresser's appointment.

Harriet You've found one then.

Dorothy In fact, no. I shall take a taxi back to Kynance, say hallo to the Kraelsheimers, and then pop in to Eduard's. He's staying open for me.

Harriet If that's what you want to do.

Dorothy I know it seems rather a long way to go for a simple blow-job, but one feels so much more relaxed in familiar surroundings.

Harriet Did you say a ——

Dorothy A blow-job.

Harriet I thought you did.

Dorothy Not original, I'm afraid. One of Jeremy's little terminologies.

Harriet I see.

Dorothy Now then, a "cu'a"?

Harriet Oh, thank you.

Dorothy You do seem rather distant today, dear. Is anything wrong?

Harriet I've told you; I have this manuscript to finish.

Dorothy Well, dear, it is your choice.

Harriet Yes, it's my choice.

Dorothy I don't suppose there's anything I can do to help?

Harriet I think perhaps not.

Dorothy I suppose it's frightfully left-wing, is it?

Harriet You would probably think so.

Dorothy I'm not a complete stranger to the subject, you know. I did actually live in those parts.

Harriet Up to a point.

Dorothy Now what does that mean? And kindly do not say, "Oh, nothing."

Harriet It means up to a point. Just that.

Dorothy I have to say, Harriet, that is sounds distinctly, well, judgemental.

Harriet Judgemental?

Dorothy Yes.

Harriet And what does that mean?

Dorothy It means that I think the matter would best be left closed pro tem. Rowing we can manage without.

Harriet Right.

Dorothy Now then, to revert to my visitor for a moment.

Harriet Yes.

Dorothy I think it only fair all round to establish that you don't mind him coming here. You would say, wouldn't you?

Harriet I'm delighted he's coming. It's been dragging on for weeks. Ever since you've been here. I thought he was going to get everything rushed through.

Dorothy He's done his damnedest; but as you know, these things are never quite as straightforward as one imagines.

Harriet No, actually. I don't know. I've never had my house burnt down. In fact I don't know anyone who's had their house burnt down.

Dorothy Then you must have led a very sheltered life.

Harriet Sheltered by whom?

Dorothy Not by whom. By what. By what you let yourself see. All that stuff. That's sheltering. That's not experience.

Harriet But you haven't even read it.

Dorothy I don't need to.

Harriet That's arrogant. That's incredibly arrogant.

Dorothy Not as arrogant as telling me, when I remind you that I have actually lived in the very region about which all that stuff is being written, that I have only lived there up to a point. As though it was only half a life. Or a quarter of a life. Or whatever fraction of a life you choose to permit. Since you seem so intimately acquainted with it, perhaps I am to conclude that I was not living my own life at all, but that you were doing it for me.

Harriet Don't accuse me of what you do.

Dorothy I am not ... dumping. I may not have the education that we made possible for you.

Harriet I thought it was the Frigger.

Dorothy Yes, for which Daddy gave a life's work. Don't imply that I have lived in cotton wool; or that I did not have plenty to do with the relatives of the Desparecedos.

Harriet Now you're going to tell me about the maid, Modesta.

Dorothy Yes, her nephew. Or that we didn't suffer nightmares of anxiety in eighty-two.

Harriet I'm not going to talk about the Falklands.

Dorothy Well, that makes a change.

Harriet Heavens, Mummy, I've never seen you flare up like this.

Dorothy I'm not flaring up.

Harriet You've lost your temper.

Dorothy We do not lose our tempers.

Harriet Silly me.

Dorothy This is justifiable anger. Now then, a "cu'a", and it's forgotten.

Harriet Have you seen any houses yet?

Dorothy Not as such, no.

Harriet Do you not think it might be wise?

Dorothy From whose point of view? I've told you, Harriet, if I am in any sense in the way ——

Harriet You are not getting in the way.

Dorothy There is apparently a very presentable property, quite compact but perfectly adequate, in Gledwyn Mews. Two down from the Marriotts.

Harriet Are you seeing it?

Dorothy I think so, dear. It is said to have belonged to one of the Norfolks' mistresses. It has a cellar which runs below the street, and also a well.

Harriet Sounds perfect.

Dorothy Not a very big well.

Harriet But a well, nevertheless.

Dorothy Once things have been sorted out with Mr Bibby, I shall go and have a look at it. On my score you need have no worries. I feel bound to say, Harriet, that my concern is rather more for you than me.

Harriet I see.

Dorothy It seems to me, a) that you have done nothing about au pairs or domestic help of any kind, b) that you are taking on far more than is good for you, and c) that — cards on the table — things are badly awry between you and Paul and that this can only have grave repercussions on the children. Well?

Harriet Well what?

Dorothy What do you have to say to that?

Harriet Nothing. You just made a statement. You said it seemed to you. Why should I start spraying my views all over the shop merely because a statement has been made?

Dorothy Your group business has made you too clever by half.

Harriet Perhaps you're jealous.

Dorothy That is displacement.

Harriet Where did you get all these words from? Surely not from Gerald?

Dorothy If we are speaking of jealousy, I would have to suggest it is yours rather than mine.

Harriet But as a family we're not jealous, remember?

Dorothy By inheritance, no. I fear it can always be acquired.

Harriet Mummy, you are not making one hundred per cent sense.

Dorothy If you are not jealous then you should be.

Harriet No, I shouldn't. I think it's the most horrible feeling in the world.

Dorothy Then be forewarned.

Harriet What is going on, Mummy?
Dorothy I think Paul might be better placed to answer that.
Harriet I didn't mean going on in ... wherever he is.
Dorothy Well, I do. And I mean in Bournemouth and Stratford and
Aberdeen as well.
Harriet Say whatever it is you want to say.
Dorothy Want? Not want to say. Not want at all. Have to say.
Harriet Say it then.
Dorothy Harriet, when did Paul last speak to you on the phone?
Harriet Two weeks ago.
Dorothy Did he mention Helen?
Harriet I can't remember. No, I don't think so. Why?
Dorothy Because these do.

*Dorothy opens her handbag and produces an envelope full of credit card
receipts*

Harriet What are those?
Dorothy American Express receipts.
Harriet Where did you get them?
Dorothy I didn't get them anywhere. They arrived.
Harriet But you opened them.
Dorothy In error.
Harriet Oh, pull the other one.
Dorothy I said, and I meant, in error. I had no idea whatsoever that you
or Paul used an American Express card — it did not seem your style —
so naturally when I saw the envelope on the hall floor I assumed that
mine had been forwarded.
Harriet Forwarded from where?
Dorothy The Kraelsheimers have been fielding my mail at Kynance.
Harriet Then there would have been handwriting on the envelope.
Dorothy Had I been wearing my reading glasses, I expect I would have
noticed that there was none. As I say, I assumed that the statement was
mine. But I hardly think that it behoves us to get bogged down in details.
Harriet You mean like Bournemouth and Stratford and Aberdeen?
Dorothy Naturally I assumed that I was being falsely billed, and so
checked further.
Harriet I don't imagine you will answer this, Mummy, but ——
Dorothy I shall do my best.

Harriet Do you expect, I mean, in your heart of hearts, really expect me to believe this?

Dorothy What you choose to do with the truth is entirely your own affair.

Harriet When did it arrive?

Dorothy This morning.

Harriet Why didn't you let me have it sooner?

Dorothy I didn't see you.

Harriet Why did you leave the rest of the mail on the floor?

Dorothy Did I?

Harriet Yes. You usually put it on the side.

Dorothy Do I?

Harriet You know you do. You couldn't wait to go through it, could you?

Dorothy I do not pretend — therefore I shall not try to convince you otherwise — that I did not read it. Had I merely returned it to you without making it clear that I had read it, having opened it in error, I think you will agree that that would have been less than honest.

Harriet What have you got, then? Good, is it?

Dorothy Hardly good. But since you ask: Aberdeen and Stratford I would say are inconclusive. Bournemouth, I'm afraid, is not.

Harriet What do you mean, inconclusive?

Dorothy I am afraid that the Bournemouth dates coincide precisely with those for which he said he was in Geneva.

Harriet He was in Geneva.

Dorothy How do you know?

Harriet He phoned me from Geneva.

Dorothy You mean you checked with the international operator?

Harriet Of course not. In fact, he phoned me twice from Geneva.

Dorothy No dear, from Bournemouth.

Harriet Then it's an error.

Dorothy I rather fear not.

Harriet They make errors. Everyone makes errors. You said you opened the damned thing in error.

Dorothy I concede that I may make errors in some departments. In others, I fear I do not.

Harriet Give it to me, please.

Dorothy The room in the Winter Gardens Hotel appears to have been a double. Not twin; double.

Harriet Give it to me, please.

Dorothy Then there was an expenditure of a hundred and eighty-four pounds, twenty pence at Paris Centrale, which is neither a station nor a restaurant, but a clothes shop. A women's clothes shop. Would that I had the wherewithal. I see no signs of such couture in your wardrobe, Harriet. Nor have I ever.

Harriet For the third time.

Dorothy Unless you have been married to a transvestite all these years.

Harriet Those statements are mine.

Dorothy In point of fact, no, they are Paul's. And very clear statements they are, too.

Harriet Give them to me.

Dorothy What do you intend to do with them?

Harriet I expect I shall follow the family line and pretend that I opened them in error.

Dorothy Except that I am not pretending.

Harriet And he would believe me about as much as I believe you.

Dorothy Do you mean there is a history of mistrust between you? I find that sad.

Harriet No, you don't. I believe you draw strength from it. You're enjoying this, aren't you?

Dorothy There are times when it would be gratifying to be proved correct. This is not one of them.

Harriet You're damned well loving it.

Dorothy It would be very easy for me, Harriet, simply to turn the other way.

Harriet Not so much fun, though.

Dorothy Gratitude I do not expect. That is not my style.

Harriet Then what is your style? What do you want?

Dorothy Merely to help.

Harriet If you really wanted to help, you'd just have left me alone. That is the only help I need. The hardest help, isn't it, because it means doing nothing and staying silent.

Dorothy But I cannot simply ignore my sense of responsibility.

Harriet But you have no right to it anymore.

Dorothy No right to it?

Harriet No. How would you like *my* help?

Dorothy Help in what, dear?

Harriet Shall I start by checking that ghastly man's briefcase to see that he carries condoms?

Dorothy I shall ignore that.

Harriet Well, shall I? Shall I check? I can easily.

Dorothy Not clever or funny.

Harriet But I'd really like to check for you. I'd feel so much happier for you if I knew everything was safe.

Dorothy This is unnecessary.

Harriet You mean you've checked already and he keeps them in his wallet?

Dorothy Harriet, I'm bound to think that perhaps you're not entirely well.

Harriet You've always liked checking for condoms. Epiphanio said you found his. Well, I might like checking for condoms as well, and now you've gone and got there before me. It's rotten of you.

The doorbell rings

Dorothy Ah, that will be Mr Bibby.

Dorothy exits to the front door and returns with Mr Bibby

So very kind of you, Mr Bibby. My daughter, Harriet.

Mr Bibby How do you do.

Harriet Bags I check him for condoms.

Dorothy Harriet.

Harriet Hands up, cock out.

Mr Bibby I beg your pardon.

Dorothy Harriet! Will you sit down and be quiet.

Mr Bibby sits

No, not you.

Mr Bibby stands

I mean Harriet.

Harriet I'm off on a condom check. Sainsbury's first.

Dorothy Please.

Mr Bibby If this is inconvenient ——

Dorothy No, not at all. It suits us perfectly well. Doesn't it, Harriet?

Harriet I'm going. (*She makes to go*)

Dorothy But Mr Bibby is here.

Harriet I know. Isn't it foul?
Dorothy We would like you to please sit down and join us.
Harriet Why me? My house didn't burn down.
Dorothy Will you kindly rally round.
Harriet Fucking well stand on your own two fucking feet.

Harriet exits

Dorothy and Mr Bibby look at each other. Dorothy wrestles some serenity from the situation by acting as though these little shows of pique are commonplace. Mr Bibby has not the first idea what he should do

Dorothy Ah, the young.
Mr Bibby So spirited.
Dorothy Well, shall we start?
Mr Bibby Of course. I shall be as brief as I can.
Dorothy A "cu'a"? I mean, would you care for some tea?
Mr Bibby Thank you, no.
Dorothy Are you sure?
Mr Bibby Quite sure, thank you.
Dorothy Very good.
Mr Bibby Now then.
Dorothy May I first take the opportunity of saying to you how truly grateful I am to you for all that you have done.
Mr Bibby I'm sorry it's not more, Mrs Cardale.
Dorothy Oh, nonsense.
Mr Bibby That is, I'm sorry it's not enough.
Dorothy Not enough?
Mr Bibby By no means enough, I'm afraid. By no means.
Dorothy Is there something the matter?
Mr Bibby In a word, yes.
Dorothy Well?
Mr Bibby I don't quite know how to say this. I have been thinking about it.
Dorothy And?
Mr Bibby I suppose I had better come straight to the point.
Dorothy Always the best approach.
Mr Bibby Mrs Cardale, it would appear that your house is not insured.
Dorothy Of course it's not insured. I haven't even bought it yet. The Kraelsheimers and I intend ——

Mr Bibby No, no. I'm not referring to any future property; I mean the one that was so unfortunately damaged.

Dorothy Damaged, Mr Bibby? It was destroyed.

Mr Bibby Yes.

Dorothy What do you mean, not insured?

Mr Bibby I'm afraid I don't seem able to find a different form of words, Mrs Cardale.

Dorothy You say appear. Perhaps you would clarify.

Mr Bibby Certainly. Let me first make absolutely sure we have got everything quite correct. Forgive me. We are talking about Kynance Terrace, W-8.

Dorothy There is no other.

Mr Bibby Number thirty-two.

Dorothy Of course number thirty-two. You came there yourself.

Mr Bibby And it is Mrs S. T. Cardale.

Dorothy For heaven's sake, yes.

Mr Bibby And your husband's name was Mr S. T. Cardale.

Dorothy If it hadn't been, I don't know how mine could have been.

Mr Bibby And the policy was home plan number ——

Dorothy Mr Bibby, there are certain pieces of information which I simply do not carry around in my head, and the number of my home insurance policy is one of them. I'm afraid I am rather odd like that.

Mr Bibby Forgive me. I am simply trying to establish whether there is any possibility at all of an error.

Dorothy An error on whose part, Mr Bibby?

Mr Bibby Anybody's. I take it I am right to assume that the property is not insured elsewhere.

Dorothy Elsewhere?

Mr Bibby Yes. That there is not another policy held with a quite separate insurance company.

Dorothy But of course not. Should there be? Is there something wrong with Allied Provident, that it needs help from elsewhere?

Mr Bibby No, no.

Dorothy Then why the question?

Mr Bibby You see, Mrs Cardale, our records show quite clearly that the policy was not renewed in June last year, despite the issue of two reminder notices, dated the sixth and the twentieth of June respectively, and therefore became void the following month — July fourth to be precise.

Dorothy In that case there has been some error.

Mr Bibby I have naturally instigated the most thorough inquiry possible, not only with the relevant clerical department, but also with our home accounts division, and must regrettably confirm that the last credit that was registered from S. T. Cardale in respect of the property at thirty-two Kynance Terrace was on May thirtieth of the previous year — a cheque submitted by post for a sum equivalent to the cost of the premium for the ensuing twelve months. After that, Mrs Cardale, I'm afraid nothing.

Dorothy What do you mean, nothing?

Mr Bibby I fear I can hardly be plainer. There were no subsequent remittances for the policy, and it was duly rendered void. It was, in a word, cancelled.

Dorothy By whom?

Mr Bibby By its own lapsing.

Dorothy In that case there has been a banker's error.

Mr Bibby It would appear that your bank was under no instruction to transfer further monies regarding the policy. If there has been some misunderstanding between your good self and your bank, it would not be my company's position to pass observation on such a matter.

Dorothy Mr Bibby, during these recent and, one need hardly add, trying weeks, your name has been a byword for quiet efficiency and good sense. Your very name has spelt reassurance.

Mr Bibby Most flattered, I'm sure.

Dorothy I now find that I have to re-appraise the situation. I fear I shall have little choice in the future but to take my custom elsewhere.

Mr Bibby We assumed you had already done so, Mrs Cardale.

Dorothy How, pray?

Mr Bibby As I say, after the issuing of the second reminder, when the policy was still not renewed ——

Dorothy It was at the time of my husband's death.

Mr Bibby The bereavement must have been most untimely.

Dorothy What happens next, Mr Bibby?

Mr Bibby As a company, we bend over backward to accommodate.

Dorothy A prospectus I do not require.

Mr Bibby Not enough reminders and we're skinflints. Too many reminders and we are accused of mothering our customers too much.

Dorothy Mothering?

Mr Bibby Yes, mothering. You can't win, can you?

Dorothy Evidently not.

Mr Bibby Mrs Cardale, strictly between these four walls ——

Dorothy Yes.

Mr Bibby After the expiry of the reminder period, we do — and this is quite unofficial — look favourably at claims where there has been a bona fide error, for quite substantial periods after non-renewal.

Dorothy Meaning what?

Mr Bibby Forty-two days.

Dorothy But that is of no use whatsoever.

Mr Bibby As I say, we do try.

Dorothy Forty-two days.

Mr Bibby This, as I think we are both aware, is a somewhat longer period. It is, in fact, in the region of three hundred and seventy days, give or take.

Dorothy But my husband had been a dependable customer of yours for ——

Mr Bibby For one year, Mrs Cardale.

Dorothy One year.

Mr Bibby Just the one. Oh, doubtless there would have been more. Years.

Dorothy Doubtless.

Mr Bibby Even stretching a point, it would be quite impossible for the company to consider you in any way ... covered.

Dorothy Are you aware of what you are saying, Mr Bibby?

Mr Bibby Only too aware.

Dorothy If I were to now pay the premium for the period which you say was ... not covered ——

Mr Bibby Quite out of the question, I'm afraid.

Dorothy But you leave me with nothing.

Mr Bibby I am told by my various masters that it would be entirely without precedent.

Dorothy As far as I am concerned my loss is without precedent.

Mr Bibby They make the point that if the rules were to be waived for one, who knows what other liabilities we might incur.

Dorothy But you are a large and responsible concern.

Mr Bibby They also point out that those without cover are statistically those who are also less likely to be vigilant in other aspects. So that ——

Dorothy Vigilant?

Mr Bibby I speak only statistically, of course.

Dorothy There was no lack of vigilance on my part.

Mr Bibby I was not suggesting that there was.

Dorothy It was quite clearly the installation of faulty wiring coming from the boiler in the basement.

Mr Bibby You say quite clearly.

Dorothy For heaven's sake, man, any fool could see that.

Mr Bibby Ah.

Dorothy What does "Ah" mean, Mr Bibby?

Mr Bibby I think our assessors are not one hundred per cent certain of that.

Dorothy Well then, they're fools. The wiring people should pay, and pay they will. I will see to it personally that they pay. Dear God, the very thought of such shoddy workmanship is intolerable. Mr Bibby, someone could have died. What are your inspectors, or whoever they are, thinking about? Is it not staring them in the face?

Mr Bibby I regret that I have had to re-assign them to another inquiry.

Dorothy Re-assign them?

Mr Bibby In fact I rather got my knuckles rapped by head office for allowing an assessment on a property which is not on our books.

Dorothy Then you should have some gumption, man. Are there no standards left?

Mr Bibby For what it is worth, Mrs Cardale, I will tell you this. In cases where there is a clear likelihood of another party's liability, our lawyers would advise us to proceed against that party. This is what we sometimes call subrogation. However, in this instance I should point out the following: firstly, such liability is, in the view of our assessors, far from clear. Secondly, as I say, my instructions are quite firmly that we must refrain from any further work on the case. And thirdly, my own enquiries do indicate that the installation company whose services were engaged have ... ceased trading.

Dorothy What, gone out of business?

Mr Bibby As I say, they have ceased trading.

Dorothy Well then, they must start again. It proves my point; their guilt is beyond question. Does everyone now stand idly by and do nothing?

Mr Bibby These enquiries are of course of an *ex gratia* nature, Mrs Cardale.

Dorothy *Ex gratia.*

Mr Bibby I mean that they are services for which you need not expect to be invoiced.

Dorothy What can I say?

Mr Bibby I require no gratification.

Dorothy If they have ceased trading and are beyond the subrogation of which you speak, then I have recourse to nothing. Is that what you are saying? That there is no agency, no machinery, no nothing. Just loss. Pure and undiluted loss.

Mr Bibby I grant you, the circumstances are unusual.

Dorothy Do you intend that remark as a comfort to me, Mr Bibby? The confirmation of my belief that these things do not happen, and that I am therefore alone? Am I to feel some sense of relief on behalf of the entire rest of the world to whom these things do not happen? Should I somehow feel privileged in having been allocated misfortune's rarity quotient? Has the cat got your tongue?

Mr Bibby Do you wish me to take these questions in order?

Dorothy Just tell me what happens next.

Mr Bibby I'm afraid I have no crystal ball, Mrs Cardale. There was one other point which I thought I should bring to your notice.

Dorothy There's more?

Mr Bibby The neighbouring properties.

Dorothy What neighbouring properties?

Mr Bibby Numbers thirty and thirty-four Kynance Terrace.

Dorothy What of them?

Mr Bibby It would appear that they have sustained some fire damage.

Dorothy They should thank their good fortune that they are still standing.

Mr Bibby It was, mercifully, what we sometimes term a tall fire.

Dorothy It was a tall house.

Mr Bibby But, as sometimes occurs on these occasions, there was some lateral generation of heat ... the adjoining walls.

Dorothy Down, are they? Both houses open to the air? Children dangling over the void, are they, clinging like grim death to the burnt-out plasterboard?

Mr Bibby There might be some liability for damage sustained.

Dorothy Only some? What a swizz.

Mr Bibby It does to some extent depend on the respective policies of the householders.

Dorothy Their policies were never to be there.

Mr Bibby There might be some liability.

Dorothy Oh, why not all, Mr Bibby? Why not a bill for a million pounds plus VAT for the walls of numbers thirty and thirty-four? Why not a life in the workhouse, Mr Bibby, grinding my repayments out of the treadmill?

Mr Bibby Mrs Cardale, I am so sorry.

Dorothy No, you're not. You're loving it, loving it. You've been looking forward to this for days. You won't mind if you don't get paid for it. You'd give up your earnings for it.

Mr Bibby I must disagree with you.

Dorothy Of course you must.

Mr Bibby I could have terminated the enquiries earlier.

Dorothy But you'd got the smell of it in your blood by then. You wanted to run it to the ground.

Mr Bibby I was merely trying to help.

Dorothy You were drawn to the prospect of seeing someone reduced to nothing at a stroke. To see their face as everything disappears. You simpering little grub.

Mr Bibby I am sorry if I cause offence.

Dorothy You probably wear Hush-Puppies and a suede-panelled cardigan. You probably have a horrid wife in a horrid, horrid little house in Sidcup.

Mr Bibby Bromley.

Dorothy You probably go bowling with friends called Reg.

Mr Bibby Mrs Cardale, I think that if you wish to call me common, you should do so plainly.

Dorothy (*having alarmed herself by her outburst*) Oh dear, I'm so sorry, Mr Bibby, that was unforgivable of me.

Mr Bibby As a matter of fact, I hate bowling.

Dorothy I do apologize. It was quite out of character.

Mr Bibby I understand, Mrs Cardale. I think perhaps I'd better be going now.

Dorothy I'm so frightfully sorry.

Mr Bibby Think no more about it. If there is anything more that I can do.

Dorothy It does look utterly grim, does it not?

Mr Bibby I think that would be an apt description, yes. However, one is from time to time blessed with a surprise.

Dorothy I fancy I have had enough surprises for a while.

Mr Bibby Help does appear.

Dorothy Does it?

Mr Bibby It is at precisely such moments that we are ready to receive the greatest help of all.

Dorothy From?

Mr Bibby From the Lord, Mrs Cardale.

Dorothy Oh, him.
Mr Bibby The one true risen Christ.
Dorothy Then it is worse even than I thought.
Mr Bibby I well remember how ill-fortune's blows had beaten me to my knees. I called out to Him ——
Dorothy Thank you, Mr Bibby, but no thank you.
Mr Bibby Oh. Right you are.
Dorothy I am no stranger to the church. When you have lived among the Latins, you know.
Mr Bibby Yes. Well then, I had best be cutting along. If there is any advice you need. In a purely personal way.
Dorothy I do appreciate it.
Mr Bibby Thank you, Mrs Cardale. Yes, Latin America. Argentina, if memory serves.
Dorothy Yes, Argentina.
Mr Bibby By all accounts a land rich in contrasts.
Dorothy Oh yes.
Mr Bibby Yes. Goodbye then, Mrs Cardale.
Dorothy Goodbye, Mr Bibby.
Mr Bibby I'll see myself out.

Mr Bibby exits

Dorothy paces about the room in anguish

Dorothy This is, of course, a nightmare. I am for the moment residing in a nightmare. Subrogation, was it? Lateral damage. Some liability. No remittance. Oh, no, no, no. A nightmare, to be sure. Oh Stewart, Stewart, Stewart. (*She stops pacing and remains still in one corner of the room*)

Gerald and Jeremy enter, too preoccupied with their own conversation to notice Dorothy

Gerald So Sideboards turns to me as if he is intending to engage me in conversation.
Jeremy How revolting.
Gerald I'm afraid I resorted to snobbery.
Jeremy This cannot have been easy.
Gerald A matter of using the profile ... so. (*He demonstrates his cold-shouldering face*)

Jeremy That's not bad, Gez.
Gerald (*seeing Dorothy*) Ah, Dorothy, *amorado*.
Dorothy Oh, hallo boys.
Gerald Have I remarked of late that you are, in point of fact, elegance personified?
Dorothy Not now, Gerald.
Gerald That you are the most *multo elegante señora* in *el mundo*?
Dorothy Please, Gerald.
Gerald You all right, poppet?
Dorothy You are very witty and good-natured, but no games at the moment. If you don't mind.
Jeremy You feeling OK, Nana?
Dorothy I'm fine, thank you.
Jeremy Fine's not allowed, remember?
Gerald You're ever so pale, Dot. Isn't she, Jeremy?
Jeremy Yeah, fiendishly.
Dorothy Am I?
Gerald I bet it's that fellow we passed on the way in.
Jeremy El wimpo with the briefcase. Has he been giving you grief, Nana?
Gerald If he's been upsetting you, he will have me to contend with.
Jeremy Me and all.
Dorothy I must go and fetch Benji from Gladstone's.
Jeremy No, you take it easy. I'll get Benji.
Dorothy It's all right. Please excuse me.

Dorothy exits

Gerald Something I said, was it?
Jeremy Dunno, mate.
Gerald Oh dear. Your Nana is not herself, I fear.
Jeremy I shouldn't let it worry you, Gez.
Gerald But it does.
Jeremy You in love?
Gerald Oh Jeremy, really.
Jeremy Only asking.
Gerald Well, I ... erm ...
Jeremy Not going red, are you?
Gerald Of course I am not going red.
Jeremy Well, people do, you know.

Gerald Perhaps.

Jeremy Nana goes red.

Gerald Does she now?

Jeremy Yeah, I can make her, by talking about you.

Gerald Bully for you.

Jeremy I'm bound to say, I find the behaviour of the old very confusing these days. Definitely gone red, Gez.

Gerald If it makes you happy, Jeremy.

Jeremy I shouldn't really be taking the mick, should I?

Gerald It's quite all right.

Jeremy No, I mean, 'cos it's not a respectful way of going on. I should know better, really. 'Specially when I think how well we all done by having you aboard.

Gerald is puzzled, unsure whether these plaudits are straight or ironic

Me as well as Nana.

Gerald Ah.

Jeremy On account of your lifetime's experience of high finance and the corporate sector.

Gerald Oh yes, that.

Jeremy Plus there's the gravitas of your mere presence in the venture. Gives it a certain bottom. The venture, Gerald.

Gerald So you're still, so to speak, going ahead, are you?

Jeremy We, Gez, we.

Gerald You and Dot, yes.

Jeremy No, we are in a we-plural situation here. You see, Nana takes the view, as I do, that we could cast our net ever so wide and still not come up with a senior executive-type who's a patch on you.

Gerald That's very flattering, I'm sure.

Jeremy Of course, while we are eager to tap your skills reservoir, we are completely mindful of the pressures that must obtain on you in the Square Mile at this time.

Gerald Yes, yes. And has she ... has Dorothy ... has there been any mention of a, that is, a ...

Jeremy Figure?

Gerald Well, ball-park estimate.

Jeremy Ooo, ball-park estimate. I like it. Obviously, various sums have come up in the course of our discussions. Enough to get started, Gez. More than enough to get started.

Gerald I must say, your Nana is highly ambitious for you.

Jeremy This is true. And maybe I'm also just a little bit ambitious for my Nana's fella.

Gerald Quite, quite. Er, you're what?

Jeremy Come on, Gez, you can level with me.

Gerald What is there to level about?

Jeremy Well, exactly. It doesn't stack up to much, does it?

Gerald I'm not sure I'm liking your tone, Jeremy.

Jeremy Yeah, yeah, yeah. "I act for so-and-so ... I handle the such-and-such account." Doesn't wash, Gez.

Gerald Are you accusing me of ——

Jeremy Not accusing you of anything.

Gerald Good.

Jeremy It's just I know porky pies.

Gerald Now wait a minute.

Jeremy It would be strange if I didn't, seeing as how I've done my own share of trading in porky pies. And while you're in the lies business, it's ever so hard to level with yourself. I know who you "act" for, Gez.

Gerald Do tell me.

Jeremy I've seen the samples.

Gerald What samples?

Jeremy And the literature.

Gerald You're making things up again.

Jeremy Now I'm not saying there's anything wrong or shameful about travelling in babywear. I mean, if someone didn't travel in babywear, then as a nation, our carpets and undersheets would be in a whole lot worse shtuck than they are at present. It's just that it doesn't have to be you that's doing the travelling.

Gerald Where did you get all this?

Jeremy Nana.

Gerald What?!

Jeremy Look at him. I'm jesting, Gez. Besides, love's blind, innit?

Gerald Are you sure about that?

Jeremy You tell me. You're in it. If Nana's in love with you, and if she hasn't seen through it, then we have to conclude that love is lumbered with a fairly major visual impairment. I think, Gez, one of *the* rules of the entrepreneuring game is that while a little bit of cards-on-the-table is all right in the matter of presentation, you've got to keep your hand well-chested in other departments.

Gerald Which means?

Jeremy Which means not flashing your line in the wrong company.

Gerald You've been snooping.

Jeremy As a family, Gerald; letters, yes ... classic steel-framed brief-cases, no.

Gerald Ah.

Jeremy Grinning up at me from the hall floor, it was, and jammed to the gunwhales with the old bum blockers.

Gerald Ah.

Jeremy It's OK, Gez, it's OK. I did have my suspicions.

Gerald You did?

Jeremy One way and another. Oh listen, Gez, it's all right. Everything's all right. In fact, I'm bound to say I rather admire the gall. It's not that I actually enjoy seeing a close relative hoodwinked, but you know what I mean.

Gerald Now listen, Jeremy, if you are suggesting that I am somehow trying to con something out of your grandmother, then I think that, well, I don't think it would be ——

Jeremy Worthy of me?

Gerald — worthy of you.

Jeremy I wasn't suggesting.

Gerald I happen to like her for herself, and I have reason to believe the feeling is mutual.

Jeremy That's just what I mean. I think you done brilliant. And I think it's sweet.

Gerald Sweet?

Jeremy Lovely. You're both so ... so ... inexperienced. Point of fact, Gez, what did, you know, go wrong, like?

Gerald Erm.

Jeremy Ain't got form, have you?

Gerald I don't follow.

Jeremy Done time.

Gerald Oh, good heavens, no.

Jeremy Little bit of a breakdown?

Gerald Listen.

Jeremy Sorry, Gez.

Gerald Things can be difficult, do you know what I mean?

Jeremy Sure.

Gerald Do you? When you have an old mother. When there's not a lot of help about.

Jeremy Yeah, she must be knocking on.

Gerald She's not. Not anymore.

Jeremy I'm sorry.

Gerald That's quite all right.

Jeremy The thing is, we've got a plan, right? And Nana is batting for it.

Gerald I don't know what to say.

Jeremy Then don't say nothing. Just accept that someone is actually investing in you. In your image. And don't keep on not crediting it, or I'll have to think you *want* to be a loser. Ain't no down side, Gez, honest. We'll let Nana know you'd be delighted to come in on it, just part-time consulting; and that way we keep your dignity up. We tell her you was thinking of scaling down the city stuff anyway on account of not being a spring chicken no more.

Gerald Thank you, Jeremy.

Jeremy Plus on account of you wanting to spend more time around her. Well?

Gerald What an unusual young man you are.

Jeremy No, I'm not. I'm like everyone else, except that I've got started younger. What matters is going for it when you get a break. Seems to me these days they won't let no-one else in without he's got courses and diplomas hanging off him. It's no good some kid thinking he can get by with a good line in patter and a double-breasted whistle from Next. Excepting in one single area.

Gerald And that is?

Jeremy Estate agents. Our venture.

Gerald But I keep telling you, they're all up the Swannee.

Jeremy And I keep telling you, only the ones that deserve to be. There's real openings if you know where to look. If you're light on your feet. You get a phone. And a desk. And some nice notepaper, stylish, but not flash. And you lease a little place with an office front, and you're in. So then you undercut the sharks and the prannocks, and you don't try to grab a fat-cat portion straight off. And you run a tight house. Straight but tight. No gazumping, no cooking the specs, no rubber rulers. And you're honest with the punters. You see a deal, and you go for that deal, and you close. Like a crocodile's jaws, you close, and it really is that simple. We're talking property here, Gez. It's washing along right there in the Wonga stream. It's like a golden fish. Maybe it dips and darts a little. But you hook it, and you hang on to it, and you're in there too and riding on that current. Like Lester-fucking-Piggott. No, well, perhaps not Lester Piggott, but you know what I mean.

Gerald I suppose I do.

Jeremy Shall I tell you something?

Gerald I believe you shall.

Jeremy The thought has kept crossing my mind that our patron ——

Gerald You mean Dot.

Jeremy Yeah, Nana. That she has done an inchy.

Gerald A what?

Jeremy An inchy. It's what we call an insurance blaze.

Gerald On her own house? She'd never.

Jeremy How do you know?

Gerald Well, it's not her style, is it?

Jeremy Nana's style is a lot more stylish than you know.

Gerald But that would not be straight, Jeremy, would it?

Jeremy On the edge, I'd say. On the edge.

Gerald Here she is now.

Jeremy No Benji.

Gerald She's not looking right.

Dorothy enters

Jeremy Hallo, Nana.

Dorothy Benji's decided to stay over at Gladstone's.

Jeremy Is that wise?

Dorothy Wise?

Jeremy It's just that I thought Mum wanted him back.

Dorothy Then she can always go and fetch him. It's her choice.

Jeremy You're the boss.

Dorothy I am not the boss. I am simply *in loco parentis*, it seems, and I say I am content for Benji to stay at Gladstone's.

Jeremy Right, Nana.

Dorothy Yes, Jeremy.

Jeremy Give.

Dorothy I beg your pardon.

Jeremy I mean, what's eating you? Please don't say nothing. Please don't say nothing, Nana.

Dorothy I have not said nothing.

Jeremy Is it el wimpo?

Dorothy I don't know what you mean.

Jeremy The little geezer going down the front steps.

Dorothy Up to a point, yes.

Jeremy Don't bottle it up, Nana. It's not good for you.

Dorothy Is that so.

Jeremy Cards on the table. Now, what's going on?

Dorothy The answer to that is that I don't know.

Gerald I'll leave the two of you alone.

Jeremy No, Gerald. No secrets, eh Nana?

Gerald No, really. Family's family. Anyway, I need to use the dog and bone. I mean phone.

Jeremy Business?

Gerald That sort of thing. May I?

Jeremy I dunno. It's not my house. Or Nana's. I'd go for it, if I were you.

Gerald Thank you.

Jeremy Mustn't be ... caught napping, eh? Napping, geddit?

Gerald winces, but Jeremy indicates by his facial expression that any fears of his status being rumbled by Dorothy are groundless

It's all right.

Gerald exits to the front hall

Now then, Nana. Share it.

Dorothy *Todo desaparacedo.*

Jeremy Come again.

Dorothy *Todo desaparacedo.*

Jeremy English I have, Nana. Spanish, however, is uno blanco. Thought you'd have sussed that by now.

Dorothy Everything has gone. I have lost everything.

Jeremy Now remember what the quack said, Nana. About bereavement and that. Three years minimum, and here's you having just chalked up one.

Dorothy No, no. Not that, Jeremy. Not Gramps.

Jeremy What, you mean the house? Yeah, I thought you were maybe coping a bit too easy there. You're bound to get a bit of delayed shock.

Dorothy No, no.

Jeremy But you've got the chance of a fresh start. Remember what you've always said. When one door closes ——

Dorothy Except that it's not just a door, is it?

Jeremy Eh?

Dorothy It's a house. A whole bloody house.

Jeremy I don't think language is a good idea, Nana.
Dorothy This is no time to joke.
Jeremy So what's a house? You weren't *that* attached to it, were you?
Dorothy Not especially, no.
Jeremy Well then.
Dorothy *No era asegurada. No era protectada.*
Jeremy Oh Jesus.
Dorothy Not insured. The Estancia was not insured; I will receive no money as a result of its destruction by fire. None at all.
Jeremy Come off it.
Dorothy Further, the company which installed the boiler which was, the er, cradle of the blaze, has ceased trading.
Jeremy But Nana. These things don't happen. There must be something one can do.
Dorothy Namely?
Jeremy Well, something. How? I mean, how?
Dorothy Do you really require all the details?
Jeremy I just want to know what happens.
Dorothy What happens to what?
Jeremy What happens to you.
Dorothy I put this to Mr Bibby.
Jeremy El wimpo. And?
Dorothy Nothing.
Jeremy Nothing?
Dorothy I lie down upon the in-tray of the Lord and wait for Him to find a window in his diary.
Jeremy I'm going to speak to Gerald.
Dorothy Why burden Gerald?
Jeremy 'Cos he's your fella, that's why. He can sing for his supper.
Dorothy He's a busy man.
Jeremy Like hell. (*He calls*) Gerald!
Gerald (*off*) Apparently R.T.Z.'s acquired a slice of the action in the holding company.
Jeremy Stop pretending to make phone calls and get your arse in here.
Gerald (*off*) OK, B.J. Must fly. Lunch soon. *Ciao.*

Gerald enters

You called?

Jeremy Now then, Gerald, rally round, 'cos Nana here has a problem.
Dorothy No, Jeremy.
Jeremy Yes, Nana.

Harriet enters, ablaze with resolution. Lettie and Jo-Jo, similarly incandescent on her behalf, follow her in

Harriet You still here?
Jeremy Who, Mum?
Harriet All of you.
Jeremy So what's with you?
Lettie We are with her. And it's "who", not "what".
Dorothy Is this some sort of delegation?
Harriet They were on their way here.
Dorothy What a coincidence.
Harriet You know perfectly well they were due.
Dorothy Do I, dear?
Harriet They are my friends, and they were invited here.
Dorothy Is that what they are?
Harriet You have yours and I have mine.
Dorothy I have to say you are sounding distinctly confrontational.
Harriet When you have your own home, I expect you will invite whomever you choose.
Jeremy Ooops.
Dorothy Goodness, Harriet, I can't tell you how like Mummy you are sounding again.
Lettie You have no right, lady.
Dorothy To what? To draw comparisons?
Lettie To do what you do.
Dorothy I have no right to do what I do. I think I must have misread you somewhere.
Lettie To do what you have been doing.
Dorothy Do you live here, even more than I had assumed was the case, that you know what it is that I have been doing?
Jo-Jo She knows perfectly well what you mean, Lettie.
Dorothy Do I?
Lettie Did you raise your daughter to deceive?
Dorothy Don't be absurd.
Lettie Does she lie?

Dorothy As a family ——
Lettie OK.
Dorothy If she is egged on to talk nonsense about family matters which really have no place before strangers ——
Harriet I see no strangers.
Lettie I heard no nonsense.
Dorothy Then it is you who are deceived.
Lettie At least, not from her.
Harriet Where's Benji?
Jeremy Kipping at Gladstone's.
Harriet Why?
Jeremy 'Cos they're mates.
Harriet That doesn't mean he has to live there.
Jeremy Gladstone not good enough?
Harriet Don't talk bilge.
Jeremy Well.
Harriet I want Benji.
Jeremy You all right, Mum?
Dorothy When work is a little less pressing, I am sure you will find you are both more available to each other. Now then, did you have a successful outing, dear?
Harriet Successful? Why successful?
Dorothy I was only asking.
Harriet Oh yes. Bags of condoms.
Gerald A "cu'a", anyone?
Jeremy This house is well dysfunctional.
Harriet (*to Dorothy*) Are you happy?
Dorothy Harriet.
Harriet Have you got what you came here for?
Jeremy Lay off her, Mum.
Lettie Whose side are you on?
Jeremy It's not a question of sides.
Lettie Why don't you stand up for your mother?
Jeremy Why don't you tell that to Mum?
Harriet Well, have you? You seemed quite happy earlier.
Dorothy Did I?
Harriet About Paul and screwing.
Dorothy Harriet, please. *Pas devant*.
Harriet *Pas devant* who? There are no *petits* left.

Dorothy I repeat, this is not the kind of conversation we hold in public.

Harriet And I repeat, I see no public.

Dorothy You know very well what I mean.

Harriet I see only people who care for our well-being.

Dorothy I find it unworthy of you that you feel the need to go and muster your lieutenants.

Harriet I have told you.

Lettie I am no lieutenant, lady.

Dorothy I am sorry, but I was not addressing you. Either of you.

Jo-Jo Could have fooled me.

Harriet All right, Jo-Jo.

Dorothy Politeness forbids.

Harriet Is that what it is?

Dorothy Bringing people in to pull your strings. To run you.

Lettie Your daughter is perfectly capable of speaking for herself.

Dorothy I do not acknowledge your remarks anymore.

Gerald A "cu'a", definitely.

Harriet About Paul and screwing.

Jeremy Mum, please leave her alone. There's something you don't know.

Harriet Less and less, Jeremy. My mother is very good at filling in the gaps in my knowledge.

Jeremy No, something else.

Dorothy Not now, Jeremy.

Jeremy But why not?

Harriet Oh, more about Paul, is it?

Jeremy No.

Harriet Have we had the Managua Hilton on the phone chasing him up for a sauna and relief supplement?

Jeremy Mum.

Harriet I think I should be told. I think you should bite the bullet and let me know, even though it hurts you more than me.

Jeremy It's about her house.

Dorothy I really did say no, Jeremy.

Harriet I don't want to hear any more about her house.

Jeremy I give up. I really do.

Lettie Promises, promises.

Harriet Mummy, why did you want me to know about Paul and Helen?

Dorothy I've told you, Harriet. To help. To make you face it.

Harriet To be kind to be cruel?

Dorothy No.

Harriet Do you think I didn't know already?

Dorothy It never occurred to me, dear.

Harriet Of course I fucking well knew.

Dorothy I'm so sorry, Harriet.

Harriet No, you're not. You're only sorry that I've seen your reasons for what they really are.

Dorothy Meaning what?

Harriet Meaning that it would justify you for having warned me against marrying a shit.

Dorothy I never called him ... that thing.

Harriet Your words were the worse for being less direct. What do you now wish me to feel?

Dorothy To feel?

Harriet Yes.

Dorothy Why all this sanctity for feeling?

Lettie Because the rest is propaganda.

Harriet Do you wish me to crawl, exhausted, into your camp and set my standard against him, too?

Dorothy I am not set against him.

Harriet Yes, you are. You're against anything that cannot be sucked in and sat on by this whole horrible family.

Dorothy That was not worthy of you, Harriet.

Harriet You're against it because you're frightened of it. You can't operate there.

Dorothy This is deranged.

Harriet The Zigger, Moisture, Biffo, the Squirrels. Married-in eunuchs and sheer bloody strangers once removed. Who *are* these people?

Dorothy That's an absurd question.

Harriet Why do you need them?

Dorothy No. Not need.

Harriet They've really got nothing to do with you.

Dorothy Not true.

Harriet With me, then.

Dorothy That is your choice.

Harriet Them and your finds and your treasures and your little men. I don't know the language, Mummy. I just don't have it. If I want to be approved of, I will not seek approval from ... the Squirrels. Who *are* the Squirrels? They are foreigners to me ... I did not pick them. And I did not pick you.

Dorothy Now that was unpleasant.

Jeremy Low blow, Mum.

Harriet Stay out of it, Jeremy, if you do not wish to do what your grandmother does. I really have had enough. The strange thing is, Mummy, that I do love Paul. In spite of everything. And I don't love him for you, or for Jeremy, or Benji, or Lettie, or Jo-Jo, or for anybody else. But for me. Now then, if you say that you loved Daddy — which you do — then please allow me the right to say that I love Paul, and let me also live in the hope of being believed.

Dorothy Rather different, Harriet.

Harriet And yes, I do mind that Helen is so much younger than me. And yes, it does hurt that she should look like me. And no, I don't pretend to know exactly what will happen, or that I can influence anything as much as I would like to believe that I can. And yes, I expect this sort of thing goes on all the time in all sorts of households.

Jo-Jo No doubt about that.

Lettie Not now, Jo-Jo.

Jo-Jo What d'you mean?

Lettie Not your turn.

Harriet Not that it makes it easier. And no, I am not ashamed to admit it. Not ashamed about any of it anymore.

Dorothy If that is how you feel, Harriet.

Harriet It is how I feel. But I also know that you have no right to it for yourself.

Dorothy Right to what?

Harriet Any of it. To my own life in my own adulthood. You can't stand my Wednesday evenings, can you, because they're closed and they're not family, and you don't know what goes on, and there's no-one to lead it to you. And you smart. Oh, how you smart; and you grow livid with fear.

Dorothy Fear of what, pray?

Harriet Fear of my friends. Of Lettie, of Jo-Jo, of Monica; my friends. The ones I picked. The ones who love me without conditions.

Dorothy If that weren't so sad, Harriet, it could almost be funny.

Lettie I see no sadness.

Harriet Because there is no purchase for your control there. No space in which your sickness can roar.

Dorothy This is adolescent.

Harriet Do you know why you came here when you lost your house?

Dorothy I should have thought that was obvious.

Harriet I mean here and not to Veronica, who lives in Richmond — safe, clean Richmond, and who has an even bigger house. And do you know why we never talk about that?

Dorothy I can only assume there is something which you wish to hide.

Harriet I shall tell you. You are barred at Veronica's.

Dorothy Oh, what tripe.

Harriet Yes, you are. You are barred. Go into the hall and phone her and ask. Turn up the room speaker to full volume so that there is no fudging.

Dorothy No games, Harriet, for pity's sake.

Lettie Not games.

Harriet I'll tell you why you are barred. You are barred because Frank knows what you do, and he will not have you doing it in his house. I repeat, you are barred.

Dorothy I am afraid you are repeating yourself, dear, which is always a sign.

Harriet Are you still very angry with Daddy?

Dorothy With Daddy? Why on earth should I be angry?

Harriet For having behaved to you like Paul is behaving to me.

Jo-Jo And Brian.

Lettie Jo-Jo.

Dorothy That is a terrible thing to say of your father. Have you no loyalty?

Harriet Loyalty to whom?

Dorothy To anyone.

Harriet You mean the family?

Dorothy But of course.

Lettie Of course.

Harriet I have at least as much as Daddy.

Dorothy What are you saying, child?

Harriet All sorts of things. That Daddy did not have his first heart attack in his hotel bedroom next to that conference centre and that it was not brought on by overwork.

Dorothy I beg your pardon.

Harriet That it did not happen the way it was fed to us, but at a brothel in the centre of Rosario. True. That he almost snuffed it on the job, that his blood was nine parts Mescal at the time, and that three girls lifted him off while the doctor was sent for. Oh yes, and that they nicked his wallet and his watch.

Dorothy How can you say these things, Harriet?

Harriet Because they are true, and because I know how much you crave accuracy. And because Bunny Galbraith was also at the brothel and later told your friend, Father Vincente. And I found out from Father Vincente.

Dorothy But how?

Harriet The usual way. The same way as you. Think about it.

Dorothy I was only wanting to spare you and Veronica.

Harriet No, you weren't. You were trying to protect your damned family mythology. You were rehearsing the lies for a wider consumption.

Dorothy Not lies.

Harriet A sort of cancer, my arse. It was no "sort of cancer" that took him off.

Dorothy It was. It was.

Harriet It was cirrhosis. His liver by the end was like a bag of dry biscuits. Any fool could read it in the whites of his eyes — I should say the yellows of his eyes — in those last miserable fibbing weeks at the Royal Free. And I never even had to steam them open.

Dorothy Why are you doing this, Harriet?

Harriet To help, of course.

Dorothy I think perhaps it is you who need the help.

Harriet I need the eyes to shed true tears at a father's funeral, and take him all in all. I need the freedom to mourn a man and not a construction. Above all, I need honesty, not shit sprayed in silver and packaged as a truffle.

Dorothy Oh, how foul.

Harriet Not a forged inheritance. And not viciousness dressed as love.

Dorothy What viciousness?

Harriet You know all about viciousness.

Dorothy Do I?

Harriet Do you think that Veronica and I didn't know?

Dorothy About what?

Harriet About you and Daddy in the bedroom.

Jeremy Oh no, Mum.

Jo-Jo Actually, Hat.

Harriet She started it. She wants bedrooms? She shall have bedrooms. Did you think we never saw you through the gaps in the hinges? You naked on all fours, with his old gas mask on. Him drunk and whipping your bare arse with his riding crop, and you wincing forward with your cries muffled and the welts showing in the moonlight? Golden days!

Pause. This last assault has proved too much for Dorothy's commendable composure. She lowers herself into a chair, abject and, apparently, defeated. Victory, if that is what it is, seems to have gone to the younger woman. Jo-Jo is affected by the ferocity of the attack, as is Jeremy. The result is a temporary paralysis. Gerald has no physical vocabulary for the situation, and is out of the house in all but fact. If Lettie is taken aback, she is not showing it, although she stops short of the triumphal. Harriet remains in the grip of her own momentum

Gerald Time to be cutting along. Really. You've obviously all got a great
   deal to discuss, so ——
Lettie Sure.
Jeremy You disappoint me, you know that?
Gerald All the same. (*He is not sure how to select his parting words, nor
   for that matter, to whom they should be addressed*)

*Harriet will have to make do without the courtesy of a proper goodbye. So,
too, in the end, will Dorothy, who remains in the stasis of true pain*

   Keep us posted, old son. About the other thing. If anything comes up.
   If there's any news. (*To Dorothy*) Erm, poppet.

*Jeremy's silence might mean that there will be no such news, or that he too
is having difficulty over the question of a goodbye*

   Er, evening, all. So kind.

Gerald exits

Harriet (*now more regretful than passionate. The quiet after the storm*)
   Golden days. The envy of all the Squirrels. Mummy, I just don't have
   the language.
Dorothy (*mustering herself with a last call on her will*) If you would
   forgive me for a moment.

Dorothy exits

Jeremy Nana ... (*He half-makes to follow his grandmother*)
Jo-Jo Best leave her.

Jeremy Mum.

Jo-Jo Just for the moment.

Harriet The propaganda, you see.

Lettie It's OK, honey.

Harriet The stuff that said golden days.

Jeremy I should talk to Nana. She's not going to run after Gerald, is she?

Jo-Jo I don't think so, no.

Harriet It really did tell such lies.

Jo-Jo Your Gran will be all right.

Jeremy How do you know that? What do you know?

Harriet And the cards on the table. They were all tricks.

Jeremy What do any of you know?

Harriet You had to use steam, you see. And Bunny Galbraith. And jacket pockets. Epiphanio's jacket.

Lettie Who's Epiphanio?

Jeremy (*shouting*) Mum!

Harriet Darling.

Jeremy Nana's house.

Harriet Yes.

Jeremy Nana's house.

Dorothy enters with a suitcase

Dorothy No, Jeremy. Thank you.

Jeremy What are you doing, Nana?

Dorothy Doing, dear?

Jeremy I mean, where are you going?

Dorothy Then you should say so.

Jeremy Where?

Dorothy I've just thrown in the barest of necessities pro tem.

Jeremy Where, Nana?

Dorothy Well, not to Veronica's, plainly.

Jeremy So?

Dorothy Why?

Jeremy Because I'm your grandson.

Dorothy It's not your responsibility.

Jeremy You can't just go.

Dorothy And yet I just came. It is my choice.

Jeremy Her house, Mum.

Dorothy No, Jeremy, you promised. I think you'll agree it's as well she didn't know, since it would have cramped her style most fiendishly.

Harriet Know what?

Dorothy Oh, nothing.

Harriet Look, you really do not have to leave this house.

Dorothy (*with a sarcasm so fulsome as to be almost indistinguishable from real gratitude*) Oh, darling, that's sweet of you. You're an absolute angel.

Harriet It's absurd just to go.

Dorothy Oh, I think there comes a time for these things. I feel sure your friends would agree. I don't suppose any of you have seen my keys about. Perhaps I left them in my room, I mean Benji's room.

Jeremy Listen, Nana, I'm getting a gaff of my own. I got plans. Why not you and me share?

Dorothy *Querido amor*, what a thought!

Jeremy I'm serious, Nana. Listen, I got good social habits these days.

Dorothy Where *can* you have acquired them, dear?

Jeremy I don't soil nothing nowhere.

Dorothy I'm delighted to hear it. Harriet, I would give you the keys back from my bunch if I could find it. As Mademoiselle Gourcuff used to say in Geneva ——

Jeremy We both pay what we can, when we get it, and we split the kitty.

Dorothy Goodness, I haven't heard that word for longer than I care to remember.

Jeremy We both got taste and style, right?

Dorothy But no money, alas.

Harriet What do you mean, no money?

Jeremy I'm coming to that, Mum.

Dorothy I think it would be better if I made my own arrangements, one way and another. Those keys perhaps, Jeremy. They might have fallen down behind something.

Jo-Jo I'll give you a hand, son.

Jeremy Not son, there's a good girl.

Dorothy It's actually quite a big bunch; far bigger than one needs these days, a-ha-ha.

Jo-Jo Come on, Lettie.

Lettie Uh?

Jo-Jo You could make yourself useful. You could ...

Jeremy Fetch Benji from Gladstone's.

Lettie Me fetch Benji?
Jeremy You could ...
Jo-Jo Just rally round, like.
Lettie But Hat.
Jo-Jo Hat's a big girl now.
Lettie What's with you, Jo-Jo?
Jo-Jo Nothing's with me. I'm trying to help.
Lettie OK.
Jo-Jo I mean, perhaps they're best alone for a moment.
Jeremy I reckon.
Jo-Jo Being as how I'm a mum myself. You know. Oh, some other time, Lettie. C'mon.

Jeremy, Lettie, and Jo-Jo exit

Harriet What does he mean, no money?
Dorothy Oh, nothing.
Harriet Share it, Mummy.
Dorothy Share it. That's it. There's really nothing to share.
Harriet All right.
Dorothy If I could just make one observation, dear. I do think that perhaps it is a mistake always to accept what other people tell you as the truth, however well-intentioned they may appear. Not always quite that simple. Oh yes, and the ... the gas mask. It was just a game, you know. Stewart and I used to call it Pink Pigs. Do you have no private games? As far as I know, it harmed no-one, even though it was doubtless very silly. I am sorry if it caused you offence. But you know, it was private. That really was private. If I am mistaken, then I am prepared to stand corrected. But I do believe I am right in saying that no-one forced your eyes to the hinges, in which you say there was a gap.

Jeremy, Lettie, and Jo-Jo enter

Jeremy hands Dorothy the bunch of keys. Dorothy begins to separate Harriet's set from her own

(*To Jeremy*) Oh, well done, dear.
Jeremy Jo-Jo found them.
Dorothy Then well done, you. And now perhaps Jeremy, you would be

sweet enough to carry my suitcase down to the main road with me so that I can hail a taxi.

Jeremy No problem, Nana.

Dorothy (*handing a set of keys to Harriet*) Well then, Harriet. Thank you so much for having me. I can't tell you how helpful it has been.

Jeremy Can I just say something?

Dorothy Of course, darling.

Jeremy Why don't the two of you just give each other a hug or something?

Dorothy I am perfectly game.

Jeremy Mum.

Harriet looks around her, as if for reassurance, or interdiction, or something. There are no signals of dissuasion. She does indeed move in the direction of her mother, while Dorothy makes as if to meet her halfway, if not more

Dorothy Although if Harriet would rather not, I fully understand.

A brief sort of embrace occurs at roughly the centre of the room. It does not qualify as a fully fledged hug, although Jeremy and Jo-Jo look as though it could almost be willed into such a state. Harriet is doing whatever is the reverse of acting on impulse. She is drawing neither triumph nor enjoyment from the moment. Dorothy is as game as her word. The clasp subsides

Lettie (*extending a hand; to Dorothy*) I wish you well, lady.

Dorothy Do you know, I believe that, in your own way, you really do. Except that it does seem, well, perhaps a little on the late side.

Jo-Jo It's never too late.

Dorothy I really meant, what with my mother being dead these past, ooo, twenty years.

Jo-Jo Well, as a matter of fact ——

Dorothy No, no. As I said to Mr Bibby only today, thank you, but no thank you.

Jo-Jo Who is Mr Bibby?

Lettie She means Gerald and she's distancing herself already, which is good.

Dorothy No, no, no, with respect. I think the matter is best left closed, or it could all start to get fearfully complicated again.

Jo-Jo Lettie. Come on.

Lettie offers no opposition and makes to follow Jo-Jo out

Jo-Jo Harriet, love, we'll speak later.
Harriet Yes. Yes, of course.

Lettie and Jo-Jo exit

Dorothy (*to Harriet*) And then A. Jones will send word from his poste restante, just to say that A. Jones is OK.
Harriet Yes.
Dorothy Oh yes, dear. Don't forget that Benji is at Gladstone's.
Harriet Right.
Dorothy Oh yes, and he's given up sugar on his Fruit 'n' Fibre, which seems to be thoroughly ... never mind. I would have told you sooner, but what with one thing and another.
Harriet Right.
Dorothy And ... I'm sure there something else. But possibly not. (*To Jeremy*) Now, if you're ready, Jeremy. I say, what fiendishly good luck to have one's own private porter.

Dorothy exits. Jeremy, following her, pauses at the door

Jeremy I'll be ten minutes, Mum.
Harriet And then we must talk.
Jeremy Just us?
Harriet Just us.
Jeremy Right. My turn next, is it?
Harriet No. Mine, I expect. My turn next.

CURTAIN

FURNITURE AND PROPERTIES

ACT I

On stage: Sofa
Chairs
Many books, including a copy of *Women Who Love Too Much*
and a copy of *My Mother Myself*
Telephone
Teapot
Teacups and saucers
Teaspoons
Plates

Off stage: Suitcases and bags. *In them:* maté tea, scones (**Dorothy** and
Harriet)
Plastic grocery bags containing various food items, including a
flan or quiche (**Lettie** and **Jo-Jo**)
Two bottles of champagne (**Gerald**)
Box of Suchard chocolates (**Gerald**)

Personal: **Gerald:** collapsible bouquet of flashing flowers (in sleeve)

ACT II

Set: Pile of manuscripts

Off stage: Papers (**Mr Bibby**)
Suitcase (**Dorothy**)
Large bunch of keys (**Jeremy**)

Personal: **Dorothy:** handbag. *In it:* envelope of credit card receipts

LIGHTING PLOT

Property fittings required: nil
Interior. The same throughout

ACT I

To open: General interior lighting

Cue 1   **Harriet: "Oh, dear God!"**   (Page 41)
          Black-out

ACT II

To open: General interior lighting

No cues

EFFECTS PLOT

ACT I

ACT II